D1575816

WITHDRAWN

NOTES FROM THE FRONTIER

BOOKS BY HUGH NISSENSON

A Pile of Stones
Notes from the Frontier

NOTES FROM THE FRONTIER

Hugh Nissenson

THE DIAL PRESS, INC.  *NEW YORK 1968*

Copyright © 1968 by Hugh Nissenson.
All rights reserved.
No part of this book may be reproduced in any form or by
any means without the prior written permission of the Pub-
lisher, excepting brief quotes used in connection with reviews
written specifically for inclusion in a magazine or newspaper.

Library of Congress Catalog Card Number: 68-14994
Design by La Liberté
Printed in the United States of America   First Printing, 1968

49,019

HX
7605
.P3
N57

for Marilyn

Summer: 1965

BEGINNING TONIGHT, the kibbutz will be on special alert. In addition to the two men who stand watch every night until dawn, twelve more will take three-hour shifts. According to Shlomo Wolfe, this is the usual precaution against Syrian infiltrators when there's no moon.

Through his binoculars, I can see the grove of cypress trees that marks the frontier, less than two kilometers away. Behind it is OP One, the United Nations Observation Post, painted blue, and just beyond that, on the slope of the hill dotted with pine trees and scrub brush, is OP Alpha, the white UN hut in Syria. It's only when the sun flashes for a moment on a window or a cloud of red dust is raised by a truck or a bus that one is aware of the towns on the heights. And even then, at this distance, the glasses reveal very little: a cluster of whitewashed houses or a wisp of smoke. The army camps, with their artillery emplacements, are completely indistinguishable among the enormous black basalt rocks. Only Tel Azazyiat, on the summit of a small hill, six kilometers away, is clearly visible: a low stone building, with a flat roof, from which 120 mm cannon fire has for years been intermittently directed against Israeli settlements all along this part of the frontier.

"Accurate too," says Wolfe in English. "Pretty good."

He ought to know. Born in Safed, about thirty kilometers southwest of here, he has been a soldier since the age of twenty-one, when he fought in the 1948 War of Independence, and he still retains the rank equivalent of lieutenant in the Israeli army's active reserve.

"I'm on tonight," he tells me, as we walk back to his room across the parched lawn.

"Oh?"

"From eight to twelve. You can come along if you like."

"I'd like to very much."

"Good. Can you handle a Mauser?"

"I don't know. I've never tried."

"It's simple. Come on and I'll show you."

His room is stifling. One of his children has left the screen door ajar, admitting a swarm of flies that light on my arms and legs to suck at the drops of sweat. I sit on the wrought-iron chair—one of the pair that he has made himself in the kibbutz machine shop in his spare time—while he rummages through the closet to get at the automatic he keeps in a canvas holster, wrapped in a webbed belt, under a pile of shirts on the top shelf.

"Here we are."

He hands me the blunt gun, with its curious receiver, shaped like a fin, that forms the trigger guard and extends forward to an inch from the muzzle.

"How do you load it?" I ask.

"Just shove the magazine in the butt and pull back the slide."

"Is this the safety?"

"That's it. Right on the slide. Flip it with your thumb. That's the way. Give it here for a moment."

He inserts the magazine with a click, unloads it again, and then slowly dismounts it while I watch.

"It's easy. First you cock the hammer, then press the slide catch, here, push the slide forward, like this, as far as it will go, and move it back and up. There, you see? The slide and the barrel come off together. Then you push the barrel forward against the spring, lift up the breech, and take the whole thing out of the slide. It's as simple as that."

"Now what?"

"Now you have to put it back together," he says. With his tongue rolled up between his lips, he resembles a child absorbed in a game. He's happy. Not because it's a gun, but a complicated piece of machinery that fascinates him. I've seen the same expression on his face while he obsessively tinkers with some component of the kibbutz's electric generator, of which he's in charge, or the motor of my rented car. Handling any machine, his thick fingers, with their wide, cracked nails, seem to have a nervous intelligence of their own.

"I'll leave it in the closet," he tells me, standing up. "You can pick it up after dinner."

If the impending alert has upset the routine of the kibbutz, neither Marilyn nor I is aware of it. We have been here now for almost a week, and the day drags on, indistinguishable from all the others, wrapped in a luminous haze of light and heat.

Four o'clock. As usual, Shlomo and his wife, Aliza, are waiting for us on the lawn, along with their ten-year-old son, Adi, who has his father's pinched nose and his mother's beautiful dark eyes, with their black, curling lashes. He greets us in his preposterous gravel voice, then dashes off to join a bunch of boys his age kicking a soccer ball around with their bare feet.

It's the time of day when the adult members of the settlement have finished work, and their children spend a few hours with them before going off to have supper in separate quarters of their own. A shout. The ball has been kicked into the trench that runs behind the infants' house, connecting it with the concrete command bunker to the right.

"What do you do with the kids?" my wife asks Shlomo.

"What do you mean?"

"When there's an emergency, like tonight?"

"Nothing."

"Don't they sleep in the shelters?"

"Not unless there's a danger of shelling."

He yawns, lying back with his hands behind his head. The ball has been retrieved by his son, who scrambles out of the trench and shouts something to the others that makes Shlomo grin and Aliza shake her head in annoyance.

"What's he say?" Marilyn asks.

"*Hara*, Arabic for crap."

The kids continue to play, while in front of their stucco bungalows their parents relax. A long day's work, beginning at five in the morning, has exhausted them, and their faces show it. The men are sunburned and healthy looking from working in the open. Without makeup, even lipstick, the women are pale, yet strangely flushed at the same time, with blotches of color on their cheeks, from the heat that has dried out their skin and given them premature wrinkles around the eyes and at the corners of their mouths.

Aliza has prepared coffee. "Where's your sister?" she asks her son, who wanders over for a piece of fruit cake she offers him from a tin.

"At Sarele's, doing homework."

"Go and ask them if they want some cake."

"They'd say no."

"How do you know?"

"They're on a diet."

"It's true," says Aliza, in English. "I forgot. At thirteen, can you imagine? Fads. Last week it was—I forget what."

In less than an hour now, it will be dark. The dazzling sunlight, as yellow as the yolk of an egg, has already begun to shift and fade, turning the Syrian mountains a faint lilac.

Rye bread, cucumbers, carrots, white cheese, a choice of one hard- or soft-boiled egg, and a little dish of sardines, washed down by a cup or two of tepid tea: supper in the communal dining hall is always the same. By seven-thirty, the huge place is jammed, resounding with voices and the clatter of silverware and Bakelite plates. On our way out, Shlomo pauses by the door to talk with David, a huge, barrel-chested man, with bristling black eyebrows, who has recently replaced him as military commander of the kibbutz. An order from Israeli GHQ, Northern Area Command, has just been received on the phone: our defenses will be reinforced by a contingent of special Border Police who will make camp in the field next to the new apple orchard.

Outside, a cool breeze has sprung up, swaying the tops of the poplar trees against a cloudless, blue-black sky, shining with innumerable stars. The mercury vapor lamps, strung on poles along the flagstone paths between the trenches, cast circles of brilliant white light, tinged with purple and green, on the chatting couples drifting up the hill toward the children's houses to put their kids to bed.

The loaded automatic thumps against my thigh. Armed with an Uzi submachine gun, made in Israel, which he carries slung over one shoulder, the muzzle pointing down, Wolfe leads the way behind the bungalows. We are in a pine grove planted as cover.

The trick, he explains in a whisper, is to make your rounds irregularly, go back on yourself, wait a while, and then move again, in the opposite direction, so that any possible infiltrator can't fix your arrival at any given spot.

We plunge on. Now and then, a diffuse light from one of the shaded windows of the rooms reaches us through the trees. Confused by the shadows, I stumble, and the branches lash at my face. Wolfe walks erect, with his left forearm raised before him, sweeping back and forth like the windshield wiper of a car. When I pause for an instant and he goes ahead, he

9

moves silently on the balls of his feet over the dry pine needles and twigs that litter the ground. And then he too suddenly stops, and kneels down on one knee, raising the faintly gleaming barrel of his gun.

"What's the matter?"

"Shhh . . ."

We have reached the edge of a field—a seemingly limitless expanse under the stars. At first I can only hear the monotonous, rhythmical drone of the cicadas and the faint rustle of the breeze in the thistles and camel-thorns dried out by the sun. Then I throw myself down on my stomach beside him.

"What is it?" I whisper. "It sounds like a truck."

"No, listen," he tells me, a finger to his lips.

The noise again, but louder, and in the distance, perhaps two hundred yards away, a moving red light which winks out and then reappears.

"That's a truck shifting gears."

"No. A command car. Nothing." Wolfe raises his voice. "The Border Police."

We wait until the sound of the engine dies away, and the red light disappears, engulfed by the darkness that has effaced the boundary between the earth and the sky. The mountains have vanished, leaving hundreds of flickering lights in the Syrian villages mysteriously suspended in space.

"There, you can see the lights in Azazyiat," says Wolfe. "And further up, Zaoura, one of their very heavily fortified villages. It's actually settled by their army. Conscripts and their families. Now look down, and to the left, straight ahead."

"It looks like a camp fire."

"That's it. That's in Nuchele, right across the border. About a year ago, fifteen of their cows wandered into our pasture."

"What happened?"

"A big discussion in our general meeting. All very ideological. About our duties as socialists to the oppressed Arab masses." His voice is filled with amused contempt. "On the other hand, returning the cows meant that somebody would have to cross the border and take a chance of being shot on sight, or worse."

"What did you do?"

"Put it to a vote. It was decided to give the cows to our police, who impounded them. But sure enough, two days later, one of their old women shows up waving a white flag. A rag tied to a stick." He laughs through his nose. "They would send an old woman. She was scared to death, shaking like a leaf; a little dried-up old hag, without a tooth in her mouth and blind in one eye. David and I spoke with her. My Arabic is pretty good. When we told her we'd given the cows away, she thanked us politely and went back. I thought that was that, but I was wrong."

"Why? What happened then?"

"That night, they made a raid. Took us completely by surprise. Set fire to the haystack, first, near the silo, to attract our attention, and in the confusion made off with fifteen of our best milkers." Another laugh. "Fair is fair . . ."

We pass the dining hall and quietly circle left, to the west, behind the children's houses, where the mercury vapor lamps cast our gigantic shadows across the dirt road, rutted by tractor treads, that leads to the orchard. All around us, a faint mist is rising from the earth. When we leap over a trench, my left hand brushes a lilac bush and comes away soaked with cold dew.

Ten o'clock. Another quick cup of coffee in the Wolfes's room, where Aliza and Marilyn have been passing the time reading old copies of *National Geographic*, to which Shlomo subscribes.

"Everything okay?" Aliza asks.

Her husband nods. Attracted by the light, a huge moth throws itself against the screen door.

"Actually, you never really get used to it," she says. "Or I should say, I never have."

She also speaks English perfectly, with the remnant of a British public school accent.

"A week or so ago," she continues, "infiltrators threw hand grenades into a chemical tank at Amatzia, near Lachish. That's down south. Luckily no one was hurt. But the next time . . ."

She offers me a cheap Israeli cigarette. The dry, loosely packed tobacco flares up and then goes out when I neglect to take another drag immediately, leaving a bitter taste in my mouth.

Shlomo and I go on with our rounds, down past the chicken coops, in which the lights burn all night, the cowshed, huge cement silo, and the block house that contains the electric generator. He goes inside for a moment to check the machinery. The throb of the engine reverberates in the air.

"In those circumstances, ideology is useless. Worse. Naive," he resumes, when we stop off at the dining hall for a drink from the water cooler near the door. "The Arabs hate us so much it's hard to believe. I know. I've seen the bodies of our men who've fallen into their hands. We're infidels to them. Foreigners and invaders . . ."

I wait for him to continue, but he silently fingers the loaded magazine stuck in his belt. It's not the first time I've heard him talk this way. And yet, he and his wife helped found this kibbutz, and have lived here, according to its strict socialist principles, for almost seventeen years.

On the path are four border policemen wearing green berets and armed with Uzis and Belgian FN's. They are chatting with two other kibbutz members on night watch: David and "the Chink," a short, fat Russian from Shanghai, who has the sleek, black hair of an Oriental and puffy eyes. Shlomo grimaces in disgust.

"Ass . . ."

We join the group as they listen to the Chink, who, as far as I can gather, is rambling on about the ambush of a group of infiltrators near here some years ago. Even his gestures—the way he sometimes bows deferentially from the waist, with his hands clasped before him—are Chinese. He has been in the country for over seventeen years, but his Hebrew is broken and ungrammatical, interspersed now and again with a mixture of Russian, English, and even Cantonese, all of which he claims to speak fluently.

The police are from North Africa. They watch him attentively, with grins on their dark faces, as he mimes the part of the story he is evidently unable to express fully in words. Or perhaps it's for comic effect. Rolling his eyes, with his hands grasped to his belly, and his mouth twisted to one side, he describes a Syrian hit with a burst of rifle fire in the stomach. Shlomo turns away.

"He enjoyed it," he says. "Every minute of it."

We have taken up positions behind the cowshed, lying on the damp grass. Behind us, in a cypress tree, an owl hoots, then, after a moment, another, from the clump of trees to our right. But the wind has died away and except for the drone of the cicadas, which has changed to a high, incessant buzz, there is complete silence. Wolfe sits up.

"It was a mistake," he says. "We should have taken a chance and tried to return the cows. You have to begin somewhere. When they raided us, they only took what was coming to them. Despite everything, they have a primitive sense of justice. If we could somehow appeal to that . . ."

His voice, like one of his gesturing hands, hangs in the air, until he shrugs and shifts the weight of his gun from his shoulder to the crook of his arm. A faint rustle in the high grass directly in front of us, perhaps fifty yards away. Wolfe throws himself flat on his stomach and releases the safety catch on his Uzi. The rustling grows louder. I lower my head. Now the cicadas have ceased.

"It's a dog," I whisper.

"Keep your head down. Be quiet."

"I can see it. It's Rama. Don't shoot. What's his name's police dog."

Hearing her name, the animal bounds toward us with a bark and then suddenly stops, to wheel around, sit down on her haunches, and gnaw at the base of her tail.

"The damn fool could have gotten her head blown off," says Shlomo. He raises his voice. "You damn fool . . ."

All morning long, the Syrians have been dynamiting in the mountains. I can see nothing, not so much as a puff of smoke, but every five minutes or so the report comes again, echoing and re-echoing in the stifling air.

It's hotter today than it's been all week. The whole northern part of the country is in the grip of a heat wave that sends the temperature soaring up to 100° in the shade. The heated, shimmering air is hard to breathe, and the gusts of dry wind, blowing from a blue-white sky, seem to emanate from the blazing sun itself. Another explosion, and another, rattles the windows in the dining hall as we sit down for lunch.

"The buggers are blasting new fortifications."

This, in English, with a German accent, from Hans Cohen, who is in charge of the kibbutz's communal orchard.

In spite of the heat that makes me lightheaded and slightly queasy, he finishes off the heavy meal and wipes his greasy plate with a piece of bread. Obviously still hungry, he glances around. There are no seconds on meat—just a single slice of beef liver—so he helps himself to a huge spoonful of congealed white rice from the aluminum bowl that serves the whole table.

Another explosion, and Shlomo and I go outside to have a look. A cloud of gray smoke, tattered by the wind on the heights, drifts down toward Tel Azazyiat. He points out the gashed red earth, resembling a suppurating wound, where last November Israeli jets bombed and strafed Syrian positions that had fired on Kibbutz Dan and the cooperative village of She'ar

Yeshuv a few kilometers down the road to the west.

"Dan was hit pretty hard. First machine gun fire, and then artillery and mortars. Four members were killed, and eight wounded. The silo, gymnasium, and children's houses were hit, and some oil tanks set on fire. She'ar Yeshuv was luckier. Nobody was hurt, but some of the houses and trees in the orchard were damaged."

The explosions continue for the rest of the afternoon. Marilyn is with Aliza, who teaches math to the fifth and sixth grades in the kibbutz school. At about two, Shlomo takes me to his room to examine his geodetic maps of the area.

"You can see our situation for yourself. The Syrian mountains are about a thousand feet above us, and their fortifications on the slopes completely dominate our settlements. They shell us anytime they like, and there's nothing we can do about it, without going to war. Have you ever been in a war?"

"No."

"You're lucky."

We're interrupted by his wife, who throws herself down on the convertible sofa and closes her eyes.

"I let the kids off early. It's too hot to concentrate."

Another explosion, but much fainter this time, as if muffled by the heavy air.

"*Shabbat shalom*," she says.

I had forgotten; today is Friday, and tonight, the eve of the Sabbath.

"Yes, and a peaceful Sabbath to you, too," I tell her, in Hebrew.

Marilyn, who has taken a shower and washed her hair, sits on the edge of her cot with a towel wrapped around her head. "Why does she stay here?" she wants to know. "It doesn't make sense. Living on the border scares her to death. The class sensed it. They were uncontrollable."

"This is her home."

"It doesn't make sense to me."

I'm not so sure. Born in Nuremberg in 1930, where her father was a famous heart specialist, Aliza was sent to England in 1938 to live with her mother's older brother, a wealthy department store owner in Leeds. Adored by her aunt and uncle, who had no children of their own, she was educated at a fine public school for girls, where she excelled in math and languages.

It wasn't until 1946 that she learned that her parents had been gassed in Auschwitz three years before. Random, vivid memories of Nazi Germany she thought she had long since forgotten came back to her: the *Weinstube*, for example, on Oberere Schneidgasse, with its oak paneling, pewter dishes hung on the walls, and in one corner, the huge green tile stove, where her father would go for a glass of white wine until the S.A. came and lounged at the round tables.

"But I'm a German," her father had told her. "I was an officer, a captain, during the war. Nothing will happen to Mama and me. As soon as it blows over—'*so wie die Sache vorüber sein wird*'—you'll come home."

Aliza wasn't sure whether or not he actually believed it. Did his three-story, fifteenth-century red brick house, with its steep gabled roof and dormer windows, just off Albrecht Dürer Strasse, mean so much to him? Or his professional reputation, as spotless as his waiting room, with the potted araucaria plant on the mahogany table? Did he really think that these things would protect him? Then why had he sent her away? She couldn't figure it out, but when she tried to imagine him as a penniless refugee, with a cardboard suitcase and one change of underwear, it was impossible. Stripped of everything, even that ridiculous plant that the maid carefully dusted once a day, he would have died. She was convinced of that. But why? Were possessions so important?

She began to realize that her uncle and aunt thought the same way. The old man owned a 1939 Bentley, which had been kept on blocks in the garage since the war because of petrol rationing. And yet, he still retained a full-time chauffeur, who suffered from gout and who, instead of being grateful for the job, cracked jokes about the old Jew in the local pub.

"Never mind," her uncle would tell her. "I can buy and sell them all."

She was astonished and humiliated. "But I gradually understood," she says. "He had lived in England forty years, but he was still considered a foreigner in a country that only tolerated or hated him. Just like Papa. They both needed to own things to make them feel secure. But I had learned my lesson in Germany. You have to live in a country of your own, among your own kind. And it's not possessions that matter, but people."

And so she became a Zionist and a socialist at the age of seventeen. Auntie and Uncle were scandalized. How had they failed? All they had ever wanted was her happiness; her eventual marriage to a Jewish boy of her own class. Now they found the bric-a-brac on her bookshelf—painted china cups and saucers, little glass horses—replaced by Herzl's *Old-New Land*, a Hebrew grammar, and mimeographed and stapled pamphlets describing life on a kibbutz.

She had joined *Habonim*, the Zionist youth movement affiliated with the Mapai Party, and after six months in a special agricultural training camp in Devon, was ready to emigrate to Palestine, then in the final, violent days of the British Mandate. It wasn't until the end of the War of Independence that

she was permitted to sail. From Haifa, she was sent
for additional training to a kibbutz in the Valley of
Israel, where she met Shlomo and his group of Sabra
—native-born Israeli—and South African veterans
who had decided to establish a settlement of their
own on the Syrian frontier.

" '*Die Sache wird vorüber sein . . .*' "

"It'll blow over . . ." With each new emergency
here—shelling, infiltration, in the flickering light of
the burning haystack, shooting sparks into the air—
she and her husband recall her father's words with a
smile, as a private joke.

Sundown, and as Marilyn and I stroll up the flagstone
path to the Wolfes's, the unmistakable murmur of
prayer from a bungalow to the left is carried toward
us in fragments across a trench by gusts of hot wind.
The cracked, singsong voice rises and falls, fades
away, and becomes audible again, and when we pause
I can see the thin, crooked figure, with a fringed
prayer shawl over his head, on the porch. It's the
Saba, or grandfather, in charge of the kibbutz house-
hold repair shop, from whom I borrowed a mop and
pail several days ago. He has lived here now for almost five years to be with his daughter and three
grandchildren. Clothed, sheltered, and fed by the
kibbutz, he insists on paying for his keep by working
a full day in the little shack near the dining hall filled

with brooms, dustbins, greasy rags, pails, boxes of nails, and worn-out sandals, hanging from hooks, which he repairs with a long, sharp knife with a curved blade.

" 'The Lord reigneth; let the earth be glad; let the many coast lands rejoice. Clouds and darkness are round about Him . . .' "

For a moment, the Hebrew words are distinct. He's reciting from the prayer that inaugurates the Sabbath. Lame in his right leg from a fractured hip, he shifts his weight. When he raises his shadowed, bearded face, framed by ear-locks, a gold tooth catches the light. He wets a forefinger with his tongue, turns a page of his prayer book and resumes, mumbling under his breath.

As we walk on, we pass his open window. In the center of his tiny room is a table, covered with a white cloth and set with a plate, a pair of candlesticks, a cup, a bottle of wine, and a loaf of bread. All alone since the death of his wife about a year ago, he must bless the candles and say the benediction over the bread and wine himself. It's a curious business. Obviously without a *minyan* here—nine other Jews who would be willing to pray with him—he is obliged to omit certain portions of the service that require responsive participation. And what does he eat? The kibbutz food isn't kosher. I must ask the Wolfes.

Three more explosions, and then nothing. The Syrians have apparently finished for the day.

"*Shabbat shalom.*"
"*Shabbat shalom.*"

As it is a special occasion, all the children will eat with their parents. Dressed in a dark green skirt and a freshly laundered white blouse, Ruthie, the Wolfes's daughter, joins us in her parents' room. She is just thirteen, small-boned and dark, with black hair, and a tiny mole on her right cheek, under the eye. Too shy to enter into our conversation, she sits with her brother on the sofa, reading a Hebrew translation of *Huckleberry Finn*. With his tongue rolled up between his lips, exactly like his father, Adi is looking at the pictures in a dog-eared copy of *Life*. When Shlomo puts a tape on his Grundig recorder, the most expensive piece of personal equipment he owns, Adi puts the magazine aside and listens with obvious delight to E. Power Biggs playing Bach's *Passacaglia and Fugue in C Minor*. Proud that the boy has an interest in music—he has composed wordless little tunes—Aliza has told us that he will shortly be given piano lessons in a nearby kibbutz.

She talks about the Saba. ". . . We bring in kosher chicken or meat twice a week from Haifa. His daughter cooks it. Do you know Rivka? The tall woman with very deep-set eyes. Her oldest daughter's in

Ruthie's class. Pretty, but with a bad complexion. The old man loves it here. After he fell and broke his hip, we begged him to stop working, but he insisted. For a while he was a shoemaker in Jerusalem. He and his wife came from Russia, I think, Kishinev. Been in the country for years, since 1905, or maybe earlier. The old lady was very nice. Died of cancer. Very religious, of course."

"Mama, shhh!" Adi tells her.

We listen to the end of the *Passacaglia,* and through the *Toccata, Adagio and Fugue in C Major.* Shlomo gets up every few minutes to fiddle with the treble and bass.

"How about a drink?" he asks me.

"Fine."

"Cognac?"

He pours out two stiff shots of "777," an Israeli "deluxe" brandy that tastes of iodine.

"*L'Chaim.*"

"*L'Chaim.* Another?"

"Just a drop."

The dining hall tables have been covered with huge white cloths and set with pairs of little candles, stuck in tin holders, which have already been lit. We sit down near the door with the Chink and his wife, Naomi, a plump Moroccan girl with pock-marked, olive skin, thick lips, and almond-shaped eyes that she keeps fixed before her on her empty plate.

A tall, bony Sabra in his middle thirties named Nat sits to her left, totally absorbed in reading *Maariv*, a Hebrew evening newspaper. His long, straight, straw-colored hair, blue eyes, and drooping blond mustache remind me of an Oxford esthete of a generation or two ago. To accentuate the impression, he mumbles when he speaks.

A shout from the far end of the room, near the kitchen, calling for order, and before everyone is settled, to the accompaniment of the scraping of chairs and coughs, a woman whom I can't see quickly reads a sentence from the Sabbath service aloud.

" 'Come, let us go to meet the Sabbath, for it is a wellspring of blessing; from the beginning, from of old, it was ordained.' "

She stops, and abruptly, in an unsteady, reedy voice, starts to sing:

> *Welcome to the Sabbath . . .*
> *Peace, Peace,*
> *Peace and joy . . .*

Nat turns a page of his paper, with his little finger in the air. The Chink giggles. Here and there, scattered through the room, a hesitant, embarrassed voice joins in, and then another, until, just before the end of the song, everyone is singing. Now, from three or four tables away, a red-haired boy of about ten mumbles a passage from a paperbacked book printed in Hebrew.

"What's he saying?" Aliza asks her husband.

"I don't know. I can't hear."

"It's from Herzl," says Ruthie, spreading a thick slice of white bread with margarine and white cheese.

"I thought you were on a diet."

'I am," she tells her mother, taking a huge bite.

The food is served from aluminum trolleys wheeled down the aisles by members in rubber aprons who have been assigned a three-month hitch working in the kitchen. Chicken soup with noodles, a single leg or breast of cold roast chicken, rice again, congealed in an aluminum pot, and as a special treat, vanilla ice cream that has already melted into a thick, lumpy soup.

"Herzl is all right," says Shlomo, in a loud voice. "But why the rest of the crap? This isn't a religious community. Why bother with something that has no meaning to anyone here?"

Memories of his childhood in Safed, in the midst of a docile Orthodox community surrounded by a majority of armed, hostile Arabs, humiliate him. The thought of the bearded Jews, with their fur-trimmed hats and yellowing books, cringing behind barricaded doors during the Arab riots of the thirties, fills him with disgust.

Aliza says nothing. From what she has told me, her own father was curiously proud of being Jewish, or at least of fulfilling the obligations he felt Judaism imposed on him. She has dim memories of the Sabbath eve in Nuremberg, when it was his custom to invite to dinner one of the Polish Jewish refugees who had flooded Germany between the wars. Somehow, illuminated by the tall, beeswax candles, the image of the beggars, with their hollow, unshaven cheeks, chapped lips, and dirty nails, has fused in her imagination with what her father was destined to become.

"I picture him, sometimes, as a *Häftling*, you know, a concentration camp inmate, with a shaved head and long, filthy fingernails, wearing those striped pajamas crawling with lice. You can't imagine what a meticulous man he was . . ."

An argument at our table; or rather, the Chink is browbeating his wife who has eaten her ice cream. "You're fat," he tells her, in English.

She keeps her eyes lowered, once in a while licking her lower lip.

Thin wisps of black smoke rise from the gutted candles. It's night again. The windows reflect the lights burning above our heads, the men and women rising from their tables in little groups. The dinner is breaking up. Just before we leave, one of the watch makes his appearance: Seymour, a beefy American with cropped prematurely gray hair and a booming voice, who has stopped by to kiss his three children goodnight. He lays his submachine gun on the table clattering the plates, cups, and aluminum bowls that have not yet been cleared away.

"*Shmirah tovah.*"

He nods, with a grin. "Have a good watch," repeated, as a kind of incantation all around. We follow him when he leaves, along with Nat, still carrying his carefully folded newspaper, the Chink, and Naomi, who have been courteously included in Aliza's invitation to have a cup of coffee on the lawn. Ruthie takes her brother off to bed.

We sprawl on blankets under the stars that seem to burn just above the tops of the trees, a row of pines planted when the settlement was first established, on the far side of the command trench. They are permanently bent from the wind that blows up from the Hula Valley to the south. Seymour passes again, waving a hand.

As though excited by the sight of the oiled gun, the Chink starts to talk in his mixture of bad English and broken Hebrew about infiltration, and then about the War of Independence, when he was thrown into the battle of Latrun, commanding the approaches to Jerusalem, just after he had arrived on an immigrant ship from Shanghai.

"No training, but nothing, you understand? A Czech rifle, some ammunition, and a new ID card, so they knew who you were if you got it. A big hill.

Machine guns on top and mortars. The Arab Legion. Very good. They open up. Everybody hits the dirt, but no training, you see, we bunch up like sheep. Blood everywhere, and shit. The stink of shit . . ."

Little bubbles of saliva have gathered in the corners of his mouth. Shlomo is right. The man obviously enjoys even the recollection of his fear, as if only those emotions related to violence have the power to move him profoundly. His wife stirs uneasily. Nat rustles his paper, but he's listening intently, twisting one end of his long mustache.

"We had the same type in our outfit during the war," says Shlomo, when the Chink and his wife have finally gone. "Useful."

' For what?" asks Nat.

"To do the dirty work, of course."

It's eleven o'clock. In the last half-hour or so, it's gotten a little cooler, or at least the dampness exuding from the earth makes it easier to breathe.

"It's true," Shlomo goes on.

Stretched out on his stomach, with a fist doubled up under his chin that restricts the mobility of his narrow face and makes him slur his words, he gives the impression of being vaguely abstracted. But we are all aware that he's speaking about the most important time of his life, during the War of Independence, when he served as an officer in the Palmach, the elite striking arm of the Jewish Defense Force.

"Very useful . . ."

He describes a young Sabra under his command during the crucial battle for Lod, on the road to Tel Aviv, during the summer of 1948. "If I saw him now, I don't think I'd know him . . . Tall, thin, sandy hair. But a born killer, who loved it.

"We were ordered to attack Lod to remove the threat to Tel Aviv from the south. It was between the first and second truce called by the UN. A complicated maneuver. A commando battalion, with an armored car, attacked first, then our brigade, from the southeast. We had a six-pounder with us, and a few shells. The enemy resistance was strong. The Arab Legion and armed Arab civilians and militia fought like hell. The commandos pulled out, but we captured the southeastern outskirts at night and managed to break into the center of town.

"It's very old, with an old church, the church of Saint George, and a mosque right next door, off the main street. We had gotten word that another truce was coming, and we were ordered not to touch any of the Christian or Muslim holy places. The UN would send in inspectors, and we had to think of world opinion.

"All very well, but there we were, in the dark, with a mass of armed Arabs who outnumbered us maybe three to one, or more, all hiding inside their houses, behind shuttered windows, or in that damn mosque. Officially they had surrendered, but we knew they were just waiting for the Arab Legion to counterattack. So we stayed up all night and sweated it out. It was too quiet. Not a sound. Eli, the kid with the sandy hair, comes up to me smelling of cologne. He's found a gallon of the stuff in an abandoned Arab shop and poured it over his head.

" 'Wolfe,' he says, 'I don't like it.' But grinning from ear to ear.

"Sure enough, at dawn, the very first light, the Arabs open up. Rifle and machine gun fire from everywhere. Four of my men go down, five. *'Itbach el Yehud!'* 'Kill the Jews.' I could hear the Arabs scream. More shots, and hand grenades, tossed from the door of that mosque. They exploded right in front of me, killing three more of my men. Two more grenades. When the smoke cleared, I got up from the street and ran back to the six-pounder. The crew had already loaded it.

" 'The mosque?' they wanted to know.

" 'The mosque,' I said. 'Fire.'

"It was point-blank range. We sent two shells through the door, and after the explosions, there was silence. For maybe a minute. Then, all at once, the Arabs poured out of their houses, with their hands up, and threw their weapons on the ground. The uprising was crushed. We had the whole town. We started sending the prisoners back to their own lines, with a safe conduct.

"Then I looked inside the mosque. The white-washed walls were all pitted and splashed with blood. There was nobody—not a soul left alive. In that comparatively small space, with the thick walls, the shells had killed everybody. Maybe twenty, twenty-five, or more. Men, women, and children. I thought to myself, I'd better get them all out, dump them somewhere on the outskirts of the town, and then wash the walls. It was a mosque. Go explain what had happened to the UN. So I gave orders fast.

"We grabbed eight Arab men who had just sur-rendered, made them carry out the bodies in blan-kets, and then washed the place clean. But then I thought, the eight. What about them? They're wit-nesses. And they'd talk too, I knew it, to the UN, to anyone who'd listen, as soon as we let them go. I can't remember one of their faces. Whether they were young, or old, or what. Just eight men, picked at ran-dom, the last to surrender, all splattered with blood. Some of them had bare feet.

" 'Well? Who volunteers?' I asked my men.

"Nobody moved. Not a muscle. They all knew what I meant, but nobody said a word.

" 'It's okay, lieutenant,' says Eli. 'I'm your man.'

32

"I looked at him. There was no expression on his face. Absolutely nothing. It was just filthy and streaked with sweat. He bent down and picked up a Bren gun with a broken tripod.

" 'All right,' I told him. 'But fast.'

" 'Don't worry about a thing. *Yellah!* Let's go,' he says in Arabic.

"They shuffled off. When I heard the burst, I didn't think of anything. And later, when the truce was declared, and because we had Lod, Tel Aviv was secure, I decided, hell, if I had to do it all over again, I would. It was necessary . . ."

A lazy day. Up at ten, a quick shower, and then a leisurely breakfast of fresh cucumbers, tomatoes, cold scrambled eggs, a dish of watery sour cream, bread, margarine, jam, and strong tea, drunk from chipped china mugs without handles. The dining room is filled with parents and children spending their Sabbath together.

According to Israeli law, Saturday is the official—and only—day of rest. Here, because the farm animals have to be fed and certain chores performed, the days off are staggered, but most of the ninety-odd members are not working today, enabling them to be with their children, who have no school.

Indolence everywhere. Hans Cohen, with his feet up on a table and his chair tipped back, is arguing with his fourteen-year-old daughter, Miriam. The fat girl—her hair even blonder than her father's—munches on a thick piece of rye bread spread with jam and tries to persuade him to take her to Horshat Tal, a national park a few kilometers down the road to the east. He stands up.

"I'd love to. You know I'd love to, darling, but I've got work to do in the orchard. Go with Mama."

"She doesn't want to," says the girl, pouring a spoonful of jam on another piece of bread.

We drive over with the Wolfes in our car.

"Is it yours?" Adi asks me from the back seat.

"The car? No. We've rented it."

"Who owns it?"

"A company in Tel Aviv."

"And you pay them?"

"That's right."

He leans forward. "Is it expensive?"

"So-so."

"Nobody needs any money on a kibbutz."

"So I understand."

"If you work, everything is free. Of course, we pay for the machines. We've got two big John Deere tractors, but they belong to everybody. Have you seen them? They're beautiful. Sometimes Daddy gives me a ride, but I've been learning to drive them myself. It's simple."

"Good for you."

He lapses into a pleased silence. There's not a tree in sight, only rolling, grassy fields, overgrown with thistles and covered with huge black basalt boulders, pitted like meteorites.

"It's what everything was like before we came," Aliza says. She peers through the windshield, spattered with the squashed bodies of insects. "The Arabs did nothing . . . nothing to the land for two thousand years."

The park is crowded. Adi leaps feet first, holding his nose, into the icy water, fed by the river Dan, one of the headwaters of the Jordan that has been dammed up to form a sizable pool. His sister follows, with her hands across her small breasts, blushing with embarrassment at her one-piece bathing suit, which she apparently feels reveals too much of her developing body. The water makes me ache.

When Shlomo, Aliza, and Marilyn have had their dip, we all sit out under an enormous gnarled oak, plagued by huge stinging horseflies attracted by our wet bodies and the moist patches of grass beneath us. Shlomo catches one on the wing, near his eye, and crushes it in his hand. Another bites me on the ankle, drawing a drop of blood. It's as hot as yesterday, and with the sun at its zenith, the tree provides no shade. There are perhaps forty of them, more than thirty feet tall, with thick, leathery leaves.

"Some say that the grove is all that's left of a huge

forest that was cut down by the Turks for firewood during the First World War," says Shlomo. "They didn't touch it because it'd always been regarded as a sacred spot. In any case, it's very, very old. Who knows, maybe originally dedicated to some Canaanite god.

"When the Hebrews conquered this part of the Galilee, most of it was given to the tribe of Naphtali, except the tel, that archaeological mound in no man's land, near OP One, which was given to the tribe of Dan. Anyway, they got into trouble there, worshiped idols, a golden calf. It's mentioned twice, in what you call in English the Book of Judges, and later in the Book of Kings . . . 'And the children of Dan set up a graven image.' "

"That's pretty good."

"I should know. It's our history."

After we return to the kibbutz and have lunch, he introduces us to Amos, a self-taught prehistorian and archaeologist who has converted a wooden shack below the dining hall into a museum for artifacts he has collected in the vicinity. He has only one good eye. His pale-blue right one is made of glass, and a faint, curved scar, like a pencil mark, runs down the same side of his face, from his temple to the corner of his mouth.

"I'm no authority on the Canaanites," he says. "But that grove is obviously very old. If—this is only

a guess, mind you, but I like to think so," he adds
with a smile, "—if the Canaanites really worshiped
there, it was probably dedicated to a local Baal, the
horned god of war and fertility. You can find figur-
ines of him in Syria and Israel carrying a thunderbolt
spear or uplifted battle mace. The horns associate
him with the bull, the symbol of sex and regenera-
tion. He was worshiped in high places, and oak
groves like Horshat Tal, with the kind of thing you'd
expect: wild singing and dancing, rites of self-
mutilation, child sacrifice, and promiscuous, very
promiscuous, fornication. It went on for a long time,
way after the Hebrew conquest. Where's my Bible?
Read . . . ah . . . Hosea 1:13," he tells Shlomo.

" 'They sacrifice upon the tops of the mountains,
and burn incense upon the hills,' " Shlomo reads
aloud, in Hebrew. " 'Under oaks . . .' "

He actually recites, rather than reads, with a
muted intensity, but the dog-eared book, covered
with black oilcloth, has absolutely no religious significance for him. He regards it solely as a source of
the Hebrew language, culture, and history. Particularly history. That his family came originally from
Warsaw is beside the point. It's the armed Jew with
whom Shlomo identifies: the ferocious conquerors of
Canaan, and those who returned here after two thousand years to reclaim what they felt was always
theirs. That's why the Bible as history is so important

to him. It is, after all, the recorded deed to the country; the documentation of its original possession by the Jews.

With his back toward me, framed by the screen door saturated with light, he is absorbed in leafing through the gilt-edged pages.

We spend the next few hours with twelve or fifteen others cleaning out littered trenches. Reinforced at the sides by sheets of corrugated iron and rusted metal arches, they are filled with trash: yellowing newspapers, magazines, tin cans, rags, and broken pine branches. Once I look up to see the Saba, who has come over to watch. He wears a black silk skullcap on the back of his head. Aliza says he's over eighty, but from a distance it's hard to believe. Apart from his lameness—that broken hip that makes him throw his weight on his left leg and slightly twist his back—he stands perfectly straight. Closer, his face resembles a corpse: the mummy of Ramses the Second, preposterously bearded, but with the same discolored, parchment-like skin, sunken eyes, high cheekbones, hollow cheeks, and missing teeth. Even his grimace in the sunlight is similar—the grin of a skull. He watches us for a few minutes and then limps back to his room, undoubtedly for the afternoon Sabbath prayer.

"It's interesting. Have you ever spoken to him?" asks Aliza, who has brought us a thermos of cold lemonade. "He says that keeping the Sabbath isn't just a commandment, but also a reminder of the Garden of Eden, and the coming of the Messiah."

"Both?"

"Yes."

"How?"

"I'm not sure."

"No work," says Shlomo, unscrewing the plastic cap of the thermos and pulling out the cork.

"No, not only that. As if everything, time itself . . ."

But rather than finish the thought aloud, she describes a circle in the air with her forefinger. I rest for a moment on the bottom of the trench. If I understand her, then, for the old man the beginning and the end of history—the Messianic Age—are identical: a time when no work is necessary because humanity is part of a universal harmony in which God's will and man's are the same. The Sabbath is a rehearsal, when he must wear his best clothes—a white nylon shirt, open at the neck, and a pair of starched khakis—feast, rest, and rejoice. Forbidden to light a fire, kill so much as a fly, break a branch from a tree, walk more than a rigorously prescribed distance, carry an object or perform any labor except to preserve human life, he must spend his time praying and studying the Bible or the Commentaries on the Law, as if suffering and death had already ceased and redemption had been achieved.

39

"In the meantime, *Arbeit macht frei,*" says Aliza.

I straighten up, but with the sun directly in my eyes it's impossible to see the expression on her face. Her voice is perfectly matter-of-fact.

She was referring to the Germans' little joke— "Work brings freedom," painted over the main gate to Auschwitz—she tells me later in her room. It was her realization that the camp existed that made her an atheist.

"Papa and Mama were religious, and so were Auntie and Uncle. In Germany and England, we always went to shul. And I prayed a good deal by myself. Until I was sixteen, I prayed every night before going to bed. There's a prescribed prayer, with the line, 'Behold, he that guardeth Israel will neither slumber nor sleep.' It has to be repeated three times. I believed it. Then, when I heard about Auschwitz, and began reading all I could about it, I realized it was a lie. That prayer, and all religion. And when I went to shul, and looked around, I saw that no one really took it seriously. There was Minnie Roth, in the next pew, who dyed her hair blue. What was she interested in? Her diamonds. Or Auntie and Uncle. The fact that they were able to donate enough money to the synagogue to be given the place of honor, under the stained glass window, next to the eastern wall.

"It wasn't entirely their fault. I understand that now. All the years of cutthroat competition in a strange land made them that way. They had started off in England as dry-goods peddlers, with packs on their backs. For years they lived on herring, black bread, and cheese, until they saved enough money to buy their first store. But it's not that way here. Not on the kibbutz. We're creating a new, completely co-operative social organism here."

At eight o'clock, we accompany her and Shlomo to the children's house to put Adi to bed.

Exasperated with our incomprehensible chatter in English, Adi dashes inside. He is more animated, more raucous than in his parents' room. Aliza has told Marilyn that he refers to the children's house as "my home."

The large, single-story bungalow containing six bedrooms, a bathroom, a classroom, a kitchen, and a central dining area with low, round tables, now cluttered with wooden blocks, stuffed animals, and boxes of crayons, is where he has been living since the age of seven and will remain until thirteen.

He strips down to his undershorts, splashes water in his face, and, since his mother is watching, takes his toothbrush down from its hook and brushes his teeth. Then, whooping at the top of his lungs, he jumps onto his cot. He shares the bedroom with two other children his own age, from his group, with whom he has been raised and educated since infancy. Composed of ten boys and girls—who now sleep in separate rooms—the group is the social unit with which he has been taught to identify, a kind of kibbutz in microcosm, where he learns the cooperative values of the larger community.

Although he is allowed some personal property—his clothes, a few toys, and books—he finds it natural to share everything else with his group whom, Aliza maintains, are in many ways closer to him than brothers and sisters in a large family.

Shlomo sits on the edge of Adi's cot, and they talk in subdued voices, their foreheads almost touching. Seymour, David, and their wives join us to put their own sons to bed. The small bedroom is full, but even with the murmur of voices it is so quiet that I can hear the buzzing of an enormous insect, the length of my little finger, crawling up the window screen. Now David is reading to his son from a book with a brightly colored picture of a mounted knight on the cover, while Seymour and his boy play Chinese checkers. A black marble rolls across the tile floor. Dressed in pink pajamas, a nine-year-old girl with straight black hair peers into the room sucking her thumb. Adi sticks out his tongue.

Half an hour later, we are sitting on one of the benches in front of the dining hall. The weekly general meeting of the kibbutz is about to be held inside. Tonight it is restricted to members, who are to be briefed on some new emergency security regulations received late this afternoon from the army.

Aliza is talking about bringing up children on a kibbutz. "We've made a complete break with the past. A new beginning . . ."

She stops with a sharp intake of breath. Marilyn springs to her feet. One of those huge insects has landed on the bench between them, buzzing its wings and spasmodically curling and uncurling its long segmented abdomen. Shlomo flicks it to the ground with his forefinger.

"We've got wolves, too," he says.

"Is that so?"

"Once in a while, anyway, down from the Syrian mountains in the winter," he tells me. "But wild boars all the time. They slash the trees in the orchard with their tusks."

"Why?"

"To knock down the apples."

The insect buzzes. "A classless society," says Aliza. "The idea . . ." Her words merge with the vibrating wings and all the inhuman sounds of the night: the rustle of the trees, the hoot of an owl, a faint scurrying in the dry grass, and beyond everything else, the silence of the sky where I recognize the Big Dipper and North Star.

"Have you ever tasted wild boar?" Shlomo asks me.

"No."

"It's not bad. Cohen shot one last year. No. Actually, the year before that. Last winter a rabid wolf . . ."

His wife is silent. Her husband's interruptions have obviously irritated her, but, for an instant, she seems transfixed by the irony implicit in his words. The new society she craves is being attempted here, on a darkened frontier still possessed by wolves, wild boars, and the oak trees of a sacred grove perhaps dedicated to a horned god more than two thousand years ago.

For the past two days, I have been totally absorbed in the real life of the kibbutz—physical labor—which dominates everything else. The cotton fields in the Hula Valley urgently need weeding, so along with fifteen of the younger members, I have been assigned there.

To beat the heat, we awake at three-thirty in the morning, have a cup of tea and a piece of bread with jam in the dining hall, are at work a little after four, and get back by one in the afternoon. The five hours of sleep a night has left me with the sensation of being on a daily binge: lightheaded, parched, gritty-eyed, aching, but filled with exhilaration when I begin work, and sodden and exhausted by the time I'm finished. My hands are blistered and swollen, the little fingers slashed from the tough stems of the weeds.

But it's almost worth it, if only to witness the

dawn day after day. Actually, the sun is already up when I awake but still behind the mountains, casting a violet light, in which no tree or building is clearly defined. The corrugated iron roof of the cowshed seems partially dissolved in the air. Then, suddenly, the rim of the sun appears and gives it substance by throwing its rectangular shadow on the ground.

And always in the utter silence—do insects sleep? —there is the first cry of a bird. This morning, at exactly five to four, it was an invisible sparrow in the silver ash behind our bungalow, joined a minute later by hundreds of swallows, crested larks, and something in the myrtle bush beside the path that makes a metallic squeak like a gardener's shears trimming a hedge.

The 24 kilometer ride down to the fields in the back of a truck covered with a canvas top is a horror. For the most part, the roads are unpaved, and in addition to the jolting the fine, white dust in the valley is stifling. In spite of the *kaffiah*, the fringed Arab headdress I've wrapped around my nose and mouth, I can only take short, shallow breaths without choking. Uri, one of the young Sabras with us, is in agony from the chronic sties on his lower lids. The kibbutz nurse has warned him to wear goggles, but he's lost them—his third pair—and sits with his hands cupped over his eyes while his blond hair turns white.

The final stretch is along a paved military road,

running right along the Syrian border, shielded by two rows of shabby eucalyptus trees, with leaves shaped like spearheads. Every hundred feet is a sand-bagged emplacement for a machine gun or mortar facing the Arab fields of wheat and barley where I have occasionally caught a glimpse of a farmer plowing up the slopes of the hills with a team of oxen. The men's faces are blurred. They wear long robes and *kaffiahs*, with *argals*, or black camel's hair rings, around their heads. Yesterday one of them glanced up as we sped by. He was bearded. With him was a young boy carrying a goatskin water bag over one shoulder.

Last January, the Syrian troops on the heights opened up on a group of Israeli workers in the cotton fields with a concentrated mortar barrage that lasted two hours. No one from the kibbutz was hurt, but in a nearby field a recent immigrant from North Africa, who raised his head, was killed instantly by a piece of shrapnel that tore away the top of his skull. In the event of any trouble, Aaron Stern has ordered us to hit the dirt, cover the backs of our heads with our hands, and remain perfectly still.

Stern is a short, stocky South African, with curly black hair and a protruding jaw, who is in charge of the kibbutz cotton crop. He and I generally work in adjacent rows. The maturing plant, with its thick, woody stem and long, palmate leaves, is easily recognizable. Everything else must be carefully pulled out, and the roots left to dry up in the hot sun.

Freed from the necessity of thinking about what we're doing, we've spent the days talking. He speaks with a slight stammer that makes him raise his upper lip and crinkle his nose whenever he gets stuck on a word. Scientific farming is a passion with him, and he knows all the facts and figures by heart. When we take a break, he repeats everything in order for me to scribble it all down in a lined pad I keep rolled up in the back pocket of my shorts.

The Hula Valley was originally a lake and a huge malarial swamp which took three years for the government to drain. By 1957, about 45,000 acres were ready for cultivation, and three years later, portions of the center of the old lake, where we are now, were divided among those border settlements in the area that were in financial trouble because of their marginal land.

"The k-kibbutz is 180 meters above sea level. This valley is about 80. All the good top soil washed down here ages ago. For the first ten years after the kibbutz was established, we worked what we had up there, anyway. We had to. There was no choice. We tried to grow a little of everything. Vegetables, co-corn, peanuts, even some co-cotton. It was no use. The yields were too low. It didn't pay. We were slowly going broke."

47

He kneels down and sifts a handful of the whitish earth through his fingers. "This stuff is g-great. Limey and rich, with a high mineral content. We've got 250 acres down here. We had the idea of trying to grow co-cotton. It had never been done before in this kind of soil, but we knew it would work. For one thing, the climate's perfect."

This land in the valley has a very high water level, and it was first thought that the cotton would be able to grow without irrigation because the plants have deep roots. Unfortunately, there was a drought the first season, and the crop withered. But because the fields are right on the border, from 50 to 100 meters away, a spring that rises in Syria and flows into Israel here has been partly diverted into irrigation canals, which are much simpler and cheaper than an elaborate system of pipes or sprinklers. Once or twice a year, when the soil needs water, Stern simply has the stream blocked by concrete barricades and diverted into the canals.

"The ground soaks up the moisture, and the water level rises high enough to reach the young roots. The permanent water table is high enough to feed matured plants."

Each row is about a thousand yards long. We bend our backs. For a while, there is something immensely satisfying in the simplicity of the work. But, invariably, as the sun climbs, the exhaustion and monotony become stupefying. A thong of my right sandal cuts into my big toe at the first joint, and a blister on my left hand has burst open. To my right, just beside me, with his painful eyes almost closed, Uri looks like he's sleepwalking. A fresh sunburn has reddened his face, and his nose is raw and peeling. Stern is silent. Fatigue, apparently, makes it harder for him to talk without stammering. And yet, he's still ahead of us all, methodically pulling up the weeds with an effortless motion that is interrupted only when he stops to examine the cotton leaves for evidence of parasites. He waves me forward and shows me a leaf that has been stripped of its green epidermis, leaving just the delicate network of brown veins.

"What did that?"

"The bloody l-larva of the night butterfly."

"What can you do about it?"

"Work, man, w-weed and spray."

He yanks up a weed with one hand, carefully shakes the soil from its roots, and tosses it aside.

At eleven-thirty, we all take a break in the shrinking shadow of the truck and gulp a mouthful of water, laced with lemon juice, from a milk can. Whitened by the dust, Stern's thick black hair resembles a wig worn by an actor made up as an old man. He's in his late thirties, from Johannesburg, where his family immigrated from Lithuania around the turn of the century. While his two brothers were per-

49

fectly content to remain in South Africa, managing their father's successful import-export business, Aaron came to Israel with his wife, Nora, in 1949, determined to join a kibbutz.

"Because of the b-blacks," he explains. "The servants, particularly, waiting on you hand and foot, who'd wash out your behind if you tell them. Bloody awful."

The servility of the natives and the willingness of the whites to be completely dependent on them became intolerable to him. "I don't know which I hated more. Does that sound strange? It's hard to understand unless you've grown up in a place like that. Begun to take the way of life for g-granted. No. Worse. Much worse. G-gotten to like it. That's the real problem, you see."

"But why settle here?"

"Because on a kibbutz, exploitation is impossible."

He glances at his wristwatch, and with a nod, signals everyone back to work under the noon sun. In a few minutes, his faded blue work shirt has turned purple under the armpits from fresh sweat.

At ten to one, we quit for the day. On the way back, along the military road, we pass a platoon of soldiers, dressed in camouflage suits and carrying automatic weapons. The burly noncom, whose bristling ginger mustache makes him look like a British sergeant-major, is wearing sandals and bright red socks. The Arabs are gone.

A ruckus in the dining hall again, at lunch, between the Chink and his wife.

"Ah, now that's different," says Stern, over his vegetable soup. "That's mutual."

"What?"

"Exploitation." He's grinning.

In a whisper, although we're way out of their earshot, he tells me that while the Chink may humiliate his wife publicly, he's actually completely under her thumb and must literally beg permission just to make a trip alone into Kiriat Shemona, the nearest town.

He puts down his spoon and rests his elbows on the table. When he speaks again, in a louder voice, but without resonance, Shlomo has pulled up a chair to his left.

"M-Morocco, China, South Africa. It's about all you can expect from us. But our k-kids . . ." He turns to me. "They're something else again. Growing up in a place like this does away with all of that. The need to dominate." He pauses again. "Or to be dominated."

Shlomo says nothing. When we finish eating, I spend the next half-hour or so with him as he works. Nat has asked him to install a drop-lamp ceiling fixture, with a frosted glass bowl, in his room.

Books everywhere, in English and Hebrew: *Capital and Other Writings*, by Marx, in the Modern Library edition, Sholem's *Major Trends in Jewish Mysticism*, his two volumes in Hebrew on Shabbtai Zvi, histories, biographies, works on Judaica, and beautiful books about Israel's wildflowers, illustrated with colored photographs and drawings.

Nat has carefully marked the spot for the lamp on the ceiling over his desk with a penciled "X." Shlomo decides to put another outlet box just below the fixture on the wall.

"It's a tricky business," he says, with pride.

"I can believe it."

With a power saber saw, he cuts a channel in the plaster from the outlet just above the floor to a place up the wall near where the new fixture is to go.

"People are people," he suddenly protests, turning off the saw for a moment. "Growing up on a kibbutz doesn't change them that much."

He goes back to work, cutting slots in the exposed wooden wall studs, with his tongue rolled up between his lips. The whine of the saw makes conversation impossible, so I sit back on the bed. Little chips of plaster and slivers of wood stick to his hair.

"Listen to me," he says, when he's finished. "The kibbutz has survived for one reason. And one only."

"What's that?"

"Because it works."

Watching him at his job makes me realize that, above all, he's enjoying a satisfying life. The kibbutz fulfills his need to work with his hands while providing complete financial security for his family.

He is busy drilling a small hole in the ceiling

when Nat arrives. Evidently appalled by the mess—Shlomo is standing on some papers strewn on his desk—he hesitates in the doorway, nervously twisting one end of his long blond mustache.

"I'll be through in about an hour."

"That's all right. Take your time."

He remains where he is. From what I understand, he's an absolutely brilliant scholar and an awful teacher whose paralyzing shyness in front of a class reduces him to delivering his lectures on Jewish history in a barely audible, toneless voice, without daring to raise his eyes. Periodically fed-up, he begs the general meeting to allow him to do manual labor in the cowshed or chicken coop—anything that will allow him time to be by himself and to read or to write an occasional monograph to be published by the Hebrew University in Jerusalem. But because the shortage of university-trained teachers on the kibbutz is so acute, permission is always refused, and he drags himself back to the classroom to be plagued by the obstreperous kids.

Still, he has lived here for over ten years. Although the women try fitfully to marry him off, he remains a contented bachelor, living a life rather reminiscent of a medieval monk surrounded by his books and manuscripts, which he writes in a minuscule Hebrew script.

"This is the toughest part," Shlomo shouts with satisfaction. "Drilling through the header at the exact point in line with the outlet hole and the hole for the new switch box."

At the bungalow, where Marilyn is hanging up some wash on a line strung across the porch.

"Have you seen today's *Jerusalem Post?*" she asks.

"No. Why?"

"One of our astronauts took a walk in space."

"No kidding."

A lizard, dragging its long tail, scuttles across the tiles at my feet and disappears beneath the wooden steps. Astronauts? It occurs to me that I haven't read a newspaper or even listened to a radio in days. Seymour, who comes from Chicago and who returned there last year to visit his mother, has told me that he's never aware of how isolated it is here until he comes back from a trip. And then for days, he's astonished at the indifference with which the kibbutz generally regards the outside world.

It's true. In all the time we've been here, we haven't heard one discussion about Israeli politics, for instance, with all of its complications. This kibbutz is affiliated with the Mapai Party, which is just one of the country's political parties that have kibbutz movements. They range ideologically all the way from the extreme left to the religious. As Mapai is the most moderate of these parties, its kibbutzim are the least sectarian. The talk here is almost exclusively concerned with everyday life. Marilyn, who fled her small home town after college to work in New York, finds the insularity both familiar and irritating. I can't say that it bothers me—as yet. I'm fascinated with the intensity of this life.

"That's because you've never lived in a town like Bellefonte, Pa.," my wife tells me.

Maybe so. But what's particularly interesting is that this is so characteristically un-Jewish; the very antithesis of the cosmopolitanism of Jewish interests in a place like New York or even Tel Aviv. It's as though the poeple here have unconsciously reverted to an earlier mode of existence, or perhaps, as Aaron Stern maintains, evolved a future one, deriving from the utopian ideal that man functions best in a small community where he can never be lost in a crowd or be cut off from the productive work that sustains him.

"Alienation, in the c-classic Marxist sense, is inconceivable here," he told me the day before yesterday, in the cotton fields. "And why? It's simple. Because everyone owns everything and shares equally in the profits from his work. Labor has finally become an end in itself, as it should be."

"And is that enough?"

"Yes, you'd think so, w-wouldn't you?" he replied, with an equivocal laugh.

Some more information at supper this evening about the Saba, from his daughter, Rivka, who tells us that the old man came here from Kishinev, a town in Bessarabia, after the famous pogrom in 1903.

"My aunt . . . his oldest sister . . . was beaten to death on the street by a Russian with a length of chain, while the police stood around and laughed. As a matter of fact, the whole thing was incited by a government-sponsored newspaper that blamed the Jews for murdering a Christian in the next town and making matzoh from his blood. The old blood accusation. On Easter Sunday, which happened to be the last day of Passover that year, the Russians went wild. At noon, when they poured out of the churches after Mass.

"At first, the mob just looted the Jewish shops and homes, but by evening they were raping and killing. Little children were thrown off roofs, or murdered by having nails hammered into their skulls. It was a miracle that my parents survived. They had just been married and were living with my grandparents in a house at the edge of town. All of them went down into the cellar and hid under a pile of potatoes and prayed. Not for survival, you understand, but to be worthy."

"Of what?" Marilyn asks.

"To die for Sanctification of the Name . . ." she

says, with bewilderment and contempt in her rather deep voice.

Another sweltering morning in the cotton fields with Aaron Stern, who works with undiminished energy in spite of the heat. For almost five years now, he's dedicated himself completely to this crop, which along with Cohen's apples and pears has put the kibbutz in the black.

"The money's damn important," he tells me. "Make no m-mistake about it. We've got to make a living. On the other hand, w-working the land together is the basis of k-kibbutz life."

And a little while later, pausing at the end of the row with an uprooted weed in his hand, "None of us is religious, as you know. Work is our religion, if anything. Our justification for being here. What we've done with the land. Draining this swamp, for instance, and ma-making it productive."

"But that's already been done."

"I know," he replies slowly. "In the last six months or so, I've been thinking about that. My job here is finished. Uri could easily take over."

"What would you like to do instead?"

"I'd like to go into agricultural management. But that would mean studying first at the Weizmann Institute in Rehovoth."

"Then why don't you?"

"That's up to the whole k-kibbutz. The general meeting would have to approve it. We're very short-handed here as it is, and it would mean my being away for two years, and, when I've finished studying, working wherever I was needed."

The kibbutz, he explains, markets its cotton through a growers' cooperative that maintains store rooms, owns the gins, runs experimental stations, and shares in spinning mills and companies that make by-products from the cotton.

"Times have changed," Aaron says. "The cooperative needs trained administrators badly, and I could do it well, I know I could. The trouble is that a lot of members here feel that physical labor is the only real service you can perform for the community. That was true fifteen or twenty ye-years ago, when we were just getting started, but not now."

After lunch, we go to his room, where he turns on a small electric fan with rubber blades that only circulates the humid air.

"In Johannesburg," he says, "when I was a kid, my family had a Bantu houseboy—a middle-aged man, with gray hair, who called me 'bass' . . . 'boss.' It was intolerable. And thrilling at the same time. You c-can't imagine how dangerous such things are, how seductive, particularly to a child. One acquires the habit of domination over others so easily. And you never really lose it. Submitting to the will of the m-majority here has never been easy for me. And yet I do it. And will. It . . ."

He hesitates. But after a moment, staring at the whirling blades of the fan, he goes on. "You see, after all these years, the desire for personal power no longer frightens me. K-kibbutz life has taught me to accept it, use it for the good of the whole c-community. Whatever happens at the general meeting, I'll always be grateful for that."

"When will it be?"

"In a c-couple of weeks, I think."

With Adi, on the orchard road, where Amos has temporarily abandoned a big red John Deere tractor.

"That has a 90 horsepower engine," the boy tells me in his husky voice.

"Really?"

' With six cylinders, and eight forward speeds."

He lovingly runs his hand over the right front tire.

"Is that what you want to do when you grow up?" I ask him. "Become a member of the kibbutz and drive a tractor?"

"Yes," he says. "And I will."

A special treat for supper tonight—halvah—one slice per person. Marilyn doesn't like it, so I share hers with Shlomo, who spreads it on a piece of bread and devours it in two bites.

Edith Cohen, the American widow in charge of the kitchen—no relation to Hans—says that in recent years at least two members of the kibbutz have left solely because they couldn't stand the food. I can believe it. There is never quite enough of anything, except perhaps bread, and the monotony is maddening. Especially serious, according to Edith, who's a trained dietitian, is the shortage of meat—animal fat—for which the eggs and cheese never completely compensate.

I'm hungry an hour or so after every meal and ravenous by bedtime. And, as far as I can see, so is everyone else. That explains all the coffee and sweets they serve in their rooms at the drop of a hat.

I feel deprived of all the extras that American life provides: the hamburgers, ice cream, good Scotch, chocolate, Coke, corned beef sandwiches, and, above all, decent cigarettes. At the same time, I'm usually so hungry that I have never enjoyed a cold hard-boiled egg so much, or that extra slice of halvah that I had tonight.

As a matter of fact, all my appetites have been sharpened, so that physical pleasure of any kind, from a hot shower after work to sex and a good sleep, is particularly enjoyable. Generally lethargic, worn out by the unaccustomed work and the heat, I crave different sensations and rejoice at the simplest things, like the clean sheet spread over the straw mattress of my cot.

Stern has told me that when he first came here, he felt much the same way. He and his wife lived near the cowshed in a canvas tent with a raised wooden floor. The rough planks under his bare feet as he climbed into his cot made him happy. At home, his room had been carpeted, but he had never bothered to feel its texture or notice its design. Here, the grain in the wood idly examined one night by the light of a kerosene lamp filled him with joy. At other times, a patch of the pale-blue sky, a handful of the arid red earth sifted through his fingers, or a burr from a camel-thorn gave him the same sensation. It was a delight in the natural world that he had never experienced in Johannesburg.

And then, assigned one hot summer day to plant some pine saplings on the rise above the dining hall, he suddenly realized that the totality of his being, even his breathing and the movement of his hands as he patted down the earth, was as essential to the tiny trees as the sunlight or the rain. Thinking about it that night, his work assumed a new—almost sacramental—significance. It was a means of participating in the creation of a land—of a whole world—that was still unfinished and in the process of becoming. He had an inkling of the meaning of redemption.

"But it wasn't enough," he says. "I worked harder than ever, in the wheatfields or planting peanuts, but sooner or later, I'd get bored. I co-couldn't help it. I wanted to do something creative. But what? On a farm, once you get things going, the rest is pretty much routine. So I waited, for almost ten years, working wherever I was needed.

"It was good discipline, but hard. Sometimes—I admit it—I thought that I was w-wasting my life, and that I ought to leave here, with my family, while I was still young. Then I'd think about the pine trees. Or, once in a while, on my way to the dining hall, I'd listen to the branches squeaking in the wind. They reminded me that what I had experienced was real. I'd helped reclaim a piece of the earth. The topsoil, on the rise, was secure, we had a windbreak for the new bungalows and a patch of shade for the k-kids. I know that doesn't sound like much, but you have to remember that this was all a wilderness, a wasteland, before we came. Little by little, year after year, we were accomplishing something together. I decided to st-stick it out, and help any way that I could. At night, I b-began studying agronomy from some books published by the US Department of Agriculture . . ."

When the Hula was drained, he was ready. An American Jew, from California, had previously suggested that cotton might be grown profitably in Israel. Stern was convinced of it. At a general meeting of the kibbutz, in the winter of 1960, he persuaded the other members to try. Put in charge of the project, he succeeded beyond anyone's expectations.

This afternoon Aliza told Marilyn about a scandal that shook the kibbutz eight or ten years ago.

Marilyn repeats it to me tonight. "The old story. A man came home unexpectedly from Haifa one night and found his wife in bed with his best friend, who was also married and the father of two kids. Nothing like that had ever happened here before. The place was in an uproar for almost a month. Finally, at a general meeting, the kibbutz voted to expel the couple for 'antisocial' behavior. Naturally, their respective families left too. It reminds me of the Smalls."

"Who're the Smalls?"

"A family in Bellefonte. He was a traveling salesman for a drug company, or something, who came home one afternoon and found his wife on the sofa in the den with a neighbor from across the street. What a stink! In the end, the two families had to leave town." She laughs. "Didn't I tell you this place was no different from a small town in the States?"

For the past ten minutes, Rama has been barking outside our door. When I step onto the porch to investigate, she responds with a long, drawn-out howl.

"What is it?" Marilyn calls out.

"Nothing. Go back to sleep."

I sit on the steps, smoking a cigarette, with the panting dog at my feet. Her ears twitch. Above us, the moon is in the first quarter, just above the horizon. The thin, pale light is sufficient to throw the western mountains into relief, but the angle of the illumination makes them appear as flat as a stage set. The dog raises her head and barks again, her whole body quivering. I crush out my cigarette and peer into the shadows. Nothing.

Amos, with whom I chatted for a few minutes after supper tonight, confessed that he too is apprehensive about the possibility of an attack by infiltrators. The night before last, he was awakened by the rattle of the venetian blinds on his partly opened window. A breeze had evidently made the slats vibrate against the glass, but his first thought, as he opened his eyes, was that it was a timing mechanism connected to a bomb that had been planted beneath his window.

"When something like that happens," he said, "you don't think about anything. The mind's a complete blank. You react automatically. Before I was half awake, I had thrown myself on the floor under the bed. When I realized what was happening, I felt like a damn fool."

He laughed, but was obviously more shaken by the incident than he admitted. Aliza has told me that during the War of Independence he lost his eye in an accident with a grenade.

The dog barks again at the figure of a man coming diagonally across the lawn from the direction of the dining hall, and then wags her tail. It's Uri, her master, who has brought her supper wrapped in a newspaper—two pounds of white cheese.

This is the last week of the school term. The older children will spend their summer vacation working around the farm for about five hours a day. Ruthie's group is busy preparing for its forthcoming Bar Mitzvah, which will take place in about two weeks. It's a ceremony derived from the traditional Jewish practice of initiating thirteen-year-old boys into the religious community. In this case, however, the emphasis, for both boys and girls, will be on their assumption of adult responsibilities in the kibbutz.

Nat is in charge of devising a special ritual for the celebration and supervising the completion of a number of special tasks set for the children. Ruthie has given me her list:

1. Write an essay on Moses—his life, influence, and philosophy.
2. Write an essay on Leonardo da Vinci.
3. Write an essay on history or geography.
4. Put in a full day of work, eight or nine hours, according to sex, in a chosen area of the kibbutz.
5. Spend a night on guard duty.

6. Complete a lesson in the fundamentals of handling a rifle.
7. Make a present for parents.
8. Take a trip alone to Haifa, make a telephone call, have lunch in a restaurant, and buy yourself a gift with money provided by the kibbutz.
9. Make a trip to a neighboring kibbutz and spend the night.
10. Learn survival by camping in a field for one night with the group.
11. Learn to properly celebrate the coming of the Sabbath with the traditional blessings and songs.
12. Teach a class of younger children literature, grammar, arithmetic, and drawing for one day.
13. Write an essay on work.
14. Learn first aid.
15. Translate an essay from English into Hebrew.
16. Make a present for the school.
17. Visit Kiriat Shemona and speak with the Mayor to learn about the problems of the new immigrants.

"What did you write about Moses?" I ask her.

"I haven't done it yet."

"Do you know what you'll say?"

"That he brought us out of Egypt and gave us a country of our own."

"What else?"

"Nothing else is as important as that."

66

"She's like her father," Aliza says later. "A perfectly cold-blooded atheist."

"Does that disturb you?" Marilyn asks.

"It does, in a way. Isn't that odd? I'm not sure why. Faith is something that all children should have, at one point—like the mumps and chickenpox."

"To make them permanently immune?"

"Yes," she laughs, putting down her coffee cup. "I suppose so. But the analogy isn't exact. It's more like falling in love. Having a crush, perhaps, on an older girl. Something utterly hopeless that for a moment, at least, transfigures the whole world . . . Does that sound silly? It's something you never forget. I know I never have. Everything was significant. The way you are, what you thought, how you acted. There was no way in which you couldn't please God, or fail him. Yes, it's exactly like being in love. One is never exactly the same after that."

After supper, outside the dining hall, the Chink relates an anecdote, in a loud voice, about a Mongol he once met near Harbin who spoke fluent Yiddish. The Mongol had learned it from the Jewish refugees escaping to China after the German invasion of Russia.

". . . This is a herdsman, you understand, a regular Genghis Khan, wearing a fur cap and a quilted jacket, riding on a shaggy pony.

" 'Ten rubles?' he says to me, in perfect Yiddish.

'You only want to give me ten rubles for that beautiful fat sheep. Don't be a schlemiel . . .' "

Even Shlomo is amused. As we walk away, he is smiling.

"Once in a while, he tells a funny story," he says. "It's about all he's good for. The perfect example of someone who joined a kibbutz because he's good for nothing else. Here all he has to do is what he's told —he works with the chickens—and he has nothing to worry about. All of his needs are taken care of. In the city, on his own, he'd starve."

When she has put Adi to bed, Aliza joins us in the room and tells us something more about the Chink's marriage.

"His wife, Naomi, was born in Rabat, Morocco. She came here with her family when she was fourteen. Primitive people, but decent. A Moroccan boy wanted to marry her, but she refused. They beat their wives as a matter of course. She wanted something better.

" 'An Ashkenazi,' she once told me. 'A European Jew. Any European Jew.' The Chink met her on a trip to Tel Aviv. No woman on the kibbutz would have him, and he was desperate for a wife. They met in a movie. Before you knew it, they were engaged. Naomi's family wanted him to pay a bride's price— it's the custom—but because he was a member of a kibbutz he had no money of his own. Certainly not a thousand pounds. It didn't make any difference to

Naomi. She had her Ashkenazi at last, and she was going to hang onto him. In the end, they ran away and were married here. The funny part of it is, they're happy.

" 'He never beats me,' she says. 'He's a little baby.' She told me that years later she met the Moroccan boy in Haifa on the street.

" 'Are you married?' she said.

" 'Oh yes. Six children. Three sons.'

" 'And do you beat your wife?' "

" 'Yes. But I swear, if it had been you, I would never have touched you.' "

In his room tonight, Nat tells me that the famous Hebrew poet, Bialik, once wrote a poem about the Kishinev pogrom entitled, "In the City of Slaughter."

" 'Great is the shame, and great is the sorrow,' " he quotes in English. " 'Which is the greater? Answer, O thou son of man.' "

"Shame?"

"Precisely. For not resisting. You might say that Kishinev was a turning point in Jewish history. The beginning of the conversion of the Jews. Less than a year later, Jewish self-defense organizations sprang up all over Russia. First in Gomel, and then in Odessa, where, during the pogrom of 1905, there was fighting in the streets. Rebellion. But not only against the Gentiles. Against God himself."

He smooths down his mustache—first one side

and then the other—with the knuckle of his fore-finger.

"Suddenly, after two thousand years, the Jews had had enough. Not all of them, or even a majority, but a significant number, nonetheless. The Zionists, particularly. Men who decided to take their fate into their own hands as if God had never existed. That's what Zionism is, you see. A metaphysical revolt."

He lights a cigarette. When he resumes speaking, little wisps of smoke accompany his words.

"I'd never heard Shlomo's story about Lod before. It's interesting. I've been thinking a great deal about it. 'It was necessary,' he says. Was it really? The slaughter of eight innocent men? In any case, it was inevitable. Once we had denied God and decided to acquire power to redeem ourselves, we were destined to become like everyone else. Murderers . . . Would you like some coffee?"

"No thanks."

"I hardly ever drink it myself. It gives me heart-burn. How about a glass of tea?"

"Fine."

"I have no lemon," he mumbles under his mustache. "Do you study the Bible in the States? Here we study it in school for eleven years. 'Justice, justice, shalt thou pursue.' "

"Deuteronomy."

"Very good. In Hebrew, we say *Devarim*. Do you know how the Holy Yehudi interpreted that?"

"No."

"He was an eighteenth-century Hasidic rabbi who lived in Lublin. 'Why is it,' he was asked, 'that the word justice is repeated twice?' 'Because,' he said, 'we ought to follow justice with justice, and not unrighteousness.' That is, unrighteousness as a means to a righteous end makes the end itself unjust."

"And is that what you think?"

"I? I don't know. I think . . . He lived in a ghetto and accepted it. It was easy for him to talk."

We've heard that a kibbutz about 50 kilometers from Haifa has been attacked by infiltrators and that two houses have been blown up, with four inhabitants wounded including two children. Amos gives me a wink when I enter the dining hall for lunch.

"The children's houses," he says, spooning up his soup. "Those bastards knew what they were doing. They'd reconnoitered the place before."

"Without being discovered?"

He winks again. "It's a cinch."

"In spite of the Border Police, the army, and the night watch?"

"It's a cinch, I tell you. There's no way to stop them."

"Then what do you do?"

"Nothing yet. It's always the same. The identical pattern every time. First a bomb or a land mine, then another, until somebody gets killed and we retaliate with mortars or artillery fire. The Arabs fire back. We both protest to the Mixed Armistice Commission of the UN, and for a while everything is quiet. Then a couple of months later, it all begins again."

His tone is neither angry nor resigned, but a curious barely repressed excitement animates his scarred face as he talks. It occurs to me that he has become habituated to danger, as to a powerful stimulant. The wink—"It's a cinch"—confirms the rumor I've heard that he frequently crosses the Syrian frontier himself, at dawn, to gather various specimens for his paleontological collection. Edith Cohen has told me that on occasion he has taken his thirteen-year-old son with him.

The news about the infiltrators means extra worry for her. In addition to being a trained dietitian, she is a child psychologist who has studied on and off in Tel Aviv for four years. One of her patients here is fourteen-year-old Miriam Cohen, Hans's daughter, who has been suffering from acute insomnia ever since the present emergency began. Obsessed by the fear of an Arab attack, she is terrified of the dark, refuses to change her clothes, and overeats voraciously. Edith has been trying to persuade her parents to have her treated by a psychiatrist in Haifa.

"They won't hear of it," Edith says. "They say she's a little high strung, but that her anxiety is perfectly natural. It *is* realistic, to a degree. All the children feel it. But in her case, it's symptomatic of something else. Something much deeper."

We're in the kitchen, after lunch, where three girls in rubber aprons and bare feet are swabbing the wooden floor with mops and soapy water.

"She's rather pretty," she goes on, "with her long blond hair, but she's convinced that she's homely. No, actually ugly, because of her turned-up nose, like her mother's, which she says makes her look like a pig. Then there are her nightmares. Terrible, sado-masochistic dreams, all involving the Arabs. Torture, rape, mutilation. The night before last she dreamed they cut off her nipples . . . It happens now and again. We have three or four others, at various ages from five to sixteen, who are more or less seriously disturbed in one way or another. Two of them have benefited from psychotherapy a great deal. Ten or fifteen years ago such treatment would have been unthinkable."

"Why?"

"On ideological grounds. Because it conflicts with the utopian ideal. Communal upbringing was supposed to do away with the neurotic personality."

"But it doesn't."

She hesitates a moment. "I'd say it depends on the parents."

Late in the afternoon, I have a glimpse of Miriam having coffee on the lawn with her parents. Puffing on a pipe, her father whispers something in his daughter's ear that makes her laugh so heartily, she begins choking on a piece of cake.

Marilyn has returned to the room with a red, unglazed clay jug filled with elongated leaves and pink flowers.

"Guess what they are?" she asks me, arranging the leaves.

"I have no idea."

"Wild dog roses and wild laurel. The laurel grows only near oak trees. Did you know that? And these little purple fruits are pressed by the Arabs for their creamy juice. I forget why."

"Who told you all that?"

"Nat. We took the car and then walked for miles. He told me all about some of the wildflowers and plants that grow around here. He's very shy with women, but once he realized I was interested, I couldn't shut him up. Not that I wanted to. These roses are very rare. We found them on a side of a hill. They grow in very dense thickets. Terrible thorns. I should have worn slacks. Look at that awful scratch on my shin. But they're worth it, don't you think? That marvelous shade of pink?"

"They're very pretty."

"We saw so much, in places you'd expect nothing could grow. An old wild hawthorne tree, with green, yellow, and red fruit that tastes something like apples. The twigs are all twisted, and the bark very coarse and ragged—horribly ugly, as though it had some loathsome disease—but it had somehow taken root between two huge basalt boulders in one of those rocky fields, and it was nice to see. I can't remember half of what we saw, but there was so much, all different, and wild and wonderful . . . Oh yes, myrtle. Lots of myrtle." She bursts out laughing. "Such a silly word."

She continues laughing, less hilariously, but, I realize, with a sensuous elation from simply contemplating the wild dog roses, which she gently lifts, one by one, with her forefinger. The flowers don't resemble roses at all, but have large, flat petals.

Entertainment tonight: a movie, shown in the dining hall and, so far as I can judge, attended by almost every adult member of the kibbutz. It's a badly scratched print of *Some Like It Hot*, starring Marilyn Monroe. Although Marilyn and I have seen it in the States, we remain with the rest, squirming on the hard chairs in the stuffy room filled with smoke, delighted at the diversion.

The Hebrew subtitles translate only the barest substance of the dialogue, and except for the Americans and the South Africans, even those proficient in English have trouble following the rapid repartee. The specifically Jewish humor escapes them entirely.

When wide-eyed Marilyn Monroe, in the saloon of a yacht, asks Tony Curtis, imitating a playboy, what that enormous sailfish is on the wall, and he replies offhandedly, "a herring," there are only scattered guffaws.

"I don't get it. What's so funny about that?" Uri asks Seymour, while the reel is being changed.

"He's a poor slob, a Jewish saxophone player, not a playboy. A herring is the only fish he knows. The first one that comes to his mind."

"So?"

"Forget it!"

A bunch of us remain for a few minutes after the film is over.

"I don't understand," Uri persists. "How did you know he was supposed to be Jewish?"

"Because Jews eat herring," Seymour tells him.

"So what? So do Russians and Norwegians."

"Look. Forget it, will you?"

On the way back to the room, at twelve-fifteen, we pass Uri on the path, armed with a Lee Enfield .303 slung over one shoulder. He is on the late watch, from midnight to 4 A.M.

"Did you really think that was funny?" he asks me.

"Yes."

"Why?"

"Because of his pretensions, as Seymour said."

"Aren't there Jews in the States who own yachts?"

"Yes, of course . . ."

He shrugs and walks off, the rifle clicking against the cartridge belt he wears around his waist. It's useless to try and explain the notion of Jewish self-deprecation. The joke is lost on him.

Friday. With Stern again, in the cotton fields. He too was on guard last night, for almost four hours, and is exhausted and depressed. He forces himself to put in a full day's work. It's only when we take a break at eleven, and he stretches out in the shadow of the truck, with his hands behind his head, that he becomes talkative, but in a weary voice and with his eyes shut, as though addressing himself.

"I'm already too old for this s-sort of thing. At thirty-seven. And I no longer feel the need, the c-compulsion, to work this way."

He rises to his feet. The sight of Uri, already back at work, weeding, prompts him to reflect.

"He does a good job and enjoys it, but that's not enough. He must try and understand. If I leave, what's to prevent him from eventually doing the s-same? Or his whole generation? The important thing is to remain on the land. C-close to the earth. To be . . . How can you c-communicate something like that? I don't think it's possible."

He wipes his sweaty face with a soiled handkerchief.

Uri and I ride back together in the truck and have lunch. It's the first time we have had an extended conversation. He tells me that he was born and raised near Petah Tikvah, on the Jordanian frontier, where his father had a truck farm.

"It didn't pay. When he died, my mother sold it and we moved to Tel Aviv, where I took a job in a shoe store on Allenby Road. I hated every minute of it. It was like being cooped up in a cage. There was no room to breathe. Then I was drafted, and I saw my chance. I volunteered for Nahal. That's the way most people become members of kibbutzim nowadays. It was perfect. Special agricultural training, the best, free of charge, and then a chance to join a frontier kibbutz, get back on a farm, where I belong. Twenty of us, ten boys and ten girls, were sent up here. Most of them couldn't take it and left. City kids, filled with idealism, but soft. You know the type. I loved it. After a year I applied for membership and was accepted at a general meeting. It was just like the old times for me, but better. Much better."

"Better than owning your own place?"

"Much. No worries. You're not alone. My father was all alone and didn't have a chance. It was too much for one man without enough capital. This is organized scientifically. Everyone working together. It's common sense."

78

After lunch, I take a walk and sit for a while in the shade of the pine trees on the rise. They are ordinary, rather scrubby Scotch pines, with stiff, twisted, bluish-green needles that rustle dryly in the warm breeze. Yet for Stern, they are a reminder of an experience that changed the whole course of his life. And like all visionaries, he is anguished by the desire to communicate the meaning of that experience which by its very nature remains almost inexpressible.

On my way back to the room, I pass Uri on the lawn playing with Rama. The dog suddenly makes a stiff-legged leap into the air to snap her jaws at a fly.

News that the town of Afula, in the southern Galilee, has been attacked by infiltrators, who blew up a house, wounding a woman and two children. Edith is very disturbed about the effect it will have on Miriam and has gone to see her after lunch.

Aliza has received a letter from an old girl friend in Leeds announcing the birth of her first son. Enclosed are two color snapshots of the baby in a crib, staring at the camera with unfocused, pale-blue eyes, and one of the large Tudor Revival house in which the family lives. The picture of the house has been taken from a bad angle on the gravel driveway. All that can be seen is the right wing, with its square-headed mullioned windows, gabled roof, and molded chimney.

"Perfectly lovely," says Aliza. "And terribly pretentious, don't you think? Almost exactly like Uncle's, with that marvelous stucco and those windows. In the dining room, I remember, we had an absolutely enormous fireplace with a wrought-iron fireback. Do you know the kind? One of those things with a wild boar carved on one side and a dog on the other, standing up on their hind legs, facing each other, over a Latin motto. *Veritace Duce.* I remember that vividly. Uncle bought it at auction in London. It was frightfully expensive, and quite hideous and wonderful."

She smiles. "It's odd, when I think of it. I had almost no trouble adjusting to the physical conditions here."

She glances around the tiny room that contains everything she owns: a convertible sofa-bed, with a foam-rubber mattress, the aluminum table, with a formica top, the bookshelves, a battered plywood cupboard with sliding doors, the Grundig tape recorder on the floor, and the chairs made by her husband in which Marilyn and I sit. To my right, the closet is partly opened. A wicker basket, nailed to the inside of the door, is piled with Shlomo's underwear and socks.

"It's because we all live the same way, you see. There's no possibility of envy." She gazes at the photo of the house. "There must be fifteen rooms, at least. Her husband's in textiles. His father's business. Very

successful . . . When Shlomo and I were married, she
wrote and asked me what he did. I found . . . It was
shameful, but I discovered that I couldn't bring myself to say he was only an electrician. I wrote back
that he was an officer in the army. Not a lie, exactly,
but . . . You see, the problem in living this way is in
remembering, or making a comparison. Yes, that,
more than anything else. Bourgeois competitiveness.
When I first came here, I thought I had been cured
once and for all. Now I know it's a constant fight. A
continual struggle."

She serves the inevitable cup of coffee and some
crumbling pieces of home-made fudge that Edith
Cohen has sent over in a cake tin.

"A little too sugary," says Aliza. "The chocolate is
too light. Cheap. Good chocolate is very expensive in
Israel. Did you know that kibbutz members get only
about fifty dollars per person for spending money
each year? Edith spends most of hers on American
cigarettes. Shlomo and I buy tapes for the Grundig.
The machine was a present from Uncle. I suppose I
should have refused. I wanted to. But almost all of us
accept little gifts now and then from our families.
The Sterns have an upright piano shipped all the way
from South Africa. Nora plays quite well. A little
extra luxury doesn't do anybody any harm, I suppose,
but we have to be careful. And now, more than ever.
We're a tiny minority. Only about three percent of
the population of Israel lives on kibbutzim anymore.

Three percent! The rest of the country has become as bourgeois as England or America."

She rises to turn on the ventilator fan in the window and allows it to blow for a moment in her face. "It's like being besieged." She turns around and picks up the snapshots that have been blown from the formica table top to the tile floor. "Besieged," she repeats, "and not only from without, but from within."

"There are enormous gaps in the fossil records of the area," says Amos. "No one knows why. The earliest prehuman remains—a tooth and two pieces of skull —come from Uaidaya, just south of the Sea of Galilee, and date back between three and six hundred thousand years. After that, there's nothing for about two hundred thousand years more until hand axes like these. I've found thousands of them within a few kilometers of here. It's what we call a bifacial cleaver. You see? Both sides of the flint block have been trimmed so that they converge and form two cutting edges and a sharp point. We're not sure who made it. Paleonthropus Palestinensis, probably. Palestine Man, who seems to have been a hybrid, or a missing link between the more primitive Neanderthals and Homo Sapiens. Some of their skeletons have been found in a cave on Mount Carmel."

"What happened to them?" Marilyn asks.

"Another mystery. They disappeared. Wiped out, perhaps, or absorbed. About thirty-five thousand years ago, the area was invaded by fully developed human beings, with a higher material culture, who replaced them. Modern man, setting a precedent . . ."

We have been in his museum, among the glass cases filled with exhibits, for almost an hour now, listening to him talk. It's only the prehistory of the region that really interests him—that tremendous span of time before the invention of writing in which the eras are delineated by a subtle change in the configuration of a hand ax, or the sudden appearance, in the Hula Valley, of elongated flint blades with almost parallel sides.

"A human hand made that," he says. "Blades like that were still being made by the American Indians less than a hundred years ago. This one, here, is about thirty thousand years old. A perfect knife for cutting hair, skinning animals, or stripping the bark from trees. Almost anything. It's as strong as steel. The Upper Paleolithic blade industry was the greatest technological invention of all time. Everything that follows is based on the development of tools like these."

He goes to the next case, set against the wall, under a window.

"As time went on, they were gradually refined. All this stuff is Mesolithic, from the Middle Stone Age, about twelve to fourteen thousand years ago. The blades are much smaller, and some of them are shaped like triangles, or even trapezoids. They're parts of composite tools with separate shafts made from wood and bone. Barbed harpoons, toothed saws, sickles.

"It was a period of transition from a food-gathering to a food-growing economy. Wild cereals—barley and wheat—were harvested and then mashed up in basalt mortars. The big one on the shelf comes from Einan, in the Hula Valley, on the shore of the old lake. It's one of the earliest permanent settlements ever discovered. No one knows where the people came from. This area was constantly being invaded by new groups with higher material cultures. Some of them even had pottery. Eventually they settled down in villages where they farmed—actually planted crops and harvested them—for the first time anywhere in the world, as far as we know."

He shows us the head of a horned animal, about the length of my forefinger, carved from bone. "I found it last winter in the orchard, near the water pump. It's Chalcolithic, from the age of copper and bronze, about 5000 B.C. The same old story. Most of northern Palestine was gradually occupied by people who knew how to work metal and carve like that. My guess is that it's a goat. We know that they had domesticated animals."

We go outside into the noon sunlight, which forces him to shield his good eye with his hand. It's odd; the faintly scarred side of his face, with the artificial eye—it's plastic, actually, not glass—and more prominently defined cheekbone, is handsomer than the other. Perhaps surgery has tightened the skin.

He tells me that he became interested in archaeology in the spring of 1948, just before the outbreak of war, when his Palmach outfit was being trained at a kibbutz a few kilometers north of here. Shards of pottery and microliths—those little flint blades—found in the fields while he was on maneuvers intrigued him. Who had made them, he wondered, and what were they for? He began to read books on the subject. The Chalcolithic Age interested him most at first —the time of the Hebrew conquest of Canaan.

"I thought, well, if we did it once, we can do it again. That sounds crazy now, I know, but at the time the thought was somehow very reassuring. We were expecting a Lebanese and Syrian invasion of the Galilee at any minute. With armor. The Syrians had Renault tanks. We were being trained to stop them with home-made Molotov cocktails."

We walk up toward the dining hall.

"Actually, the Hebrews got here very late," he says, "and were only an insignificant part of a pattern that had been set hundreds of thousands of years before and was continued afterward, in historic times, by the Egyptians, Hyksos, Philistines, Greeks, Romans, Arabs, Crusaders, Turks, Jews, British—and half a dozen others I've forgotten. There's been technical progress, of course, the development of material cultures, and the ideologies that reflect them, but essentially it's the same story again and again."

We have lunch. He morosely chews a stringy slice of beef liver, swallows a mug of water, and returns to his workshop adjacent to the museum, where he spends the rest of the Sabbath cleaning hand axes encrusted by limestone with a dilute solution of hydrochloric acid and a toothbrush.

A bad scare for Rivka this afternoon. She found her father unconscious in his room, with a volume of the Mishnah on the floor beside him. For the last year or so, he has been suffering from dizziness and brief fainting spells, which a doctor from Safed has diagnosed as cardiac arrhythmia, or irregular beating of the heart. This time, however, it took his daughter and the kibbutz nurse, a buxom, pretty girl by the name of Esther Kramer, more than five minutes to bring him around. Rivka was terrified that he had again fractured his hip, but the old man swallowed a digitalis pill, impatiently waved her aside, and went back to his studies, a commentary on the meal-offering mentioned in Leviticus.

"There's really nothing that can be done," she

tells us, "except for the digitalis and a salt-free diet. It's his age."

All through supper and later, in her room, she talks about her father, unable to think of anything else.

For years, after bringing his wife to Palestine in 1905, he managed to eke out a living as a day laborer in the vineyards of Rishon Lezion, one of the earliest Zionist settlements in Palestine. In Kishinev, he had been a clerk in the office of a timber merchant. Here, pruning the vines in the hot sun almost broke him. But he got used to it and was happy. As time went on, his wife presented him with five daughters and got fat.

The dazzling blue sky and whitewashed houses made from mud, the date palms and grapes were as he had always imagined them from reading the Bible. On Saturdays and holidays, he prayed in the synagogue on Rothschild Street, cluttered with wheelbarrows, pruning hooks, and a wooden plow. Forbidden by the Turkish authorities to worship publicly, the Jews had disguised the building as a warehouse.

After the outbreak of the First World War, the Turkish army confiscated food from the civilian population. Typhus broke out in the cities and famine was widespread. In 1915, there was a plague of locusts. The old man remembers spending two days and nights in the vineyards killing the insects with a flail. But it was useless. They devoured everything, even the leaves of the little lemon tree he had planted behind his two-room house. All that remained to eat was a jar of olives and a few loaves of unleavened Arab bread.

"We went to Egypt," says Rivka. "On a neutral Spanish ship. Yossel, a cousin of my mother's, who'd lived there for three or four years, arranged the papers and sent us the tickets. Papa protested, but he had no choice.

"We lived in Cairo. Yossel had a jewelry shop in the Old Jewish Quarter, and Papa helped out. Things went very well. After a while, we were able to afford to rent a little two-story house with a courtyard. My mother decided never to go back to Palestine.

"I don't think we would have either, if my baby brother had lived. He was born a month after the war ended and died of dysentery about a month after that. Papa was inconsolable, crazy with grief. He had always wanted a son. All of a sudden, he got it into his head that the body had to be buried in the Holy Land. It was an obsession. Yossel and Mama tried to talk him out of it. The country was devastated by the war and was under military occupation. A flu epidemic was raging. Getting permission to transport the body would take months.

"He refused to listen. On the morning of the funeral, he told Mama to wrap the body up in swaddling clothes, put it in a cradle, and come with him. She obeyed. The look in his eyes terrified her. Then he packed a suitcase and took her down to the railway station and got on a train. It was the old line that ran from Cairo to Kantara, in Egypt, and then on to Haifa, I think it was, in Palestine. They went first class, figuring that the police would be less likely to bother them. My older sister, Chana, and I saw them off. I remember that the compartment had seats with white cushions.

"A couple of weeks later, Chana got a letter telling her to bring us all to Tel Aviv. Yossel was furious. 'He's crazy, crazy,' he kept shouting. But by the time we arrived, Papa seemed his old self again. The look in his eyes was gone, but his beard was completely gray. He never mentioned the baby again, but once a year he goes to the cemetery to pray over the grave. It's in Tel Aviv, near Allenby Road."

In the orchard, where I have been transferred, the apple trees have dropped some of their immature fruit. The grass is strewn with Jonathans, Delicious, San Jacintos, and Grand Alexanders that have already begun to rot in the sun, attracting swarms of bees.

"It's the June drop," Hans Cohen explains. "A natural adjustment between the amount of fruit on a branch and the amount that can be carried to maturity."

All morning long, with long-handled, two-handed shears, we prune the excess branches and then smear the wounds with white lead paint to prevent fungus infection.

Lunch is the best I've had so far on the kibbutz: scrambled eggs, cooked over a kerosene stove, thick slices of rye bread with strawberry jam, and mugs of strong, steaming tea, brewed in a tin pot by Chaim, a hired laborer from Kiriat Shemona. He is a bearded, strikingly handsome Moroccan of about forty, with magnificent white teeth, who has worked in the kibbutz orchard since coming to Israel in 1950.

"A good type," says Cohen, when we return to work. "*Echt*. Do you know German? Genuine. Intelligent, hard-working, and reliable. By now, he knows almost as much about the orchard as I do. Pears are his big specialty.

"Naturally he's religious—there's nothing I've been able to do about that—but he's come a long way. Five, no, six children, including four daughters, and they're all in high school. Do you know what it means for your average Moroccan to send his daughters to school?"

He saws on a thick branch and allows it to break off by its own weight so as not to tear the bark.

"Hired labor has always been against our principles. It's exploitation, pure and simple, but with the manpower shortage here, we have no choice. We must be practical. The least we can do is try and educate them."

Shlomo tells me something about the founding of the kibbutz. "The Jewish National Fund bought the land in 1946 from a big Arab landowner in the Galilee by the name of Kemal Effendi. He was sympathetic to the Jews. Some say it was because he had a Jewish mistress in Tiberias. In any case, he was in Lebanon during the War of Independence where he was murdered by Arab terrorists for being a traitor to their cause. They hacked him to pieces.

"After the war, a bunch of us who had fought together in the Palmach joined up with a group of South Africans from *Habonim* and came up here to settle. It was rough going for years and a lot of people left. Once in a while, we'd get a new lot from the Youth Movement but most of them didn't stay for very long. But those of us who did are glad."

Ravenous for a piece of meat, Marilyn and I drive into Kiriat Shemona for supper. It is only 5 kilometers or so from the kibbutz, and yet, an entirely different world. This is a town built for new immigrants who live in the scores of white concrete apartment buildings—hideous stucco boxes, with tiny windows—that dot the slopes of the cliff above us.

Down below, where we park our car on the main road that leads into Tiberias, is a new shopping center: a colonnaded arcade, with two banks, a café, a kosher butcher shop, buzzing with flies, a shoe store, a grocery, and, at the far end, a cavernous restaurant, jammed with customers. There are bearded Yemenites, Moroccans in caftans, Eastern Europeans wearing shabby, double-breasted suits, and sunburned Sabras, dressed in open-neck, short-sleeve shirts, khaki slacks, and sandals. The hubbub is astonishing: Hebrew, Arabic, and Yiddish, even Rumanian.

We order steak, medium rare, French fries, salad, two bottles of cold beer, and a pack of American cigarettes—Pall Malls—for which I pay the equivalent of a dollar and seventy-five cents. While we wait to be served, the lights go on in all the stores, which remain open for business until nine or ten, and the large square slowly fills up with shoppers or people out for a breath of fresh air. Most of them appear to be Jews from the Arab countries—Morocco, Tunisia, and Iraq. A bearded old Moroccan hobbles by, leaning on a stick, muffled up in a hooded djellaba. Half hidden by a column of the arcade, a young Moroccan, wearing tight blue jeans and pointed white Italian shoes, talks with a girl. When he leans forward, I catch a glimpse of his face: the long sideburns, hooked nose, clipped mustache, and gold-capped front teeth that momentarily glint in the light. The girl wears a tight green sweater and has rollers in her hair, wrapped in tissue paper. Behind her, and a little to the left, is a turbaned Kurd, a very old man, with a long white beard that covers his chest.

We eat. The meat is atrocious—tough and taste-less, fried almost to a crisp and soaked in grease. Yet we finish it all, even the yellow fat. It's the only beef we've had in weeks. With an American cigarette to smoke as I sip my beer, I'm content.

Later, when we return to the kibbutz, Aliza shows me a draft of the essay on Moses that Ruthie is writing for her Bar Mitzvah:

The repressive Egyptian feudal system needed a cheap supply of labor, which the Hebrews pro-vided. They farmed the land and helped build the pyramids and temples. Originally primitive nomads, they had no class solidarity. Moses organ-ized them. Brought up in the Pharaoh's court, he was educated and had a higher culture, like Herzl in comparison with the eastern European Jewish masses. Moses made the Hebrews class conscious and aware that they were being oppressed. Even after the Exodus, some Hebrews still had the slave mentality. They wanted to return to the flesh-pots of Egypt. Moses had them killed. To the end of his life, he taught them that in order to be free and make a nation out of themselves, they had to be class conscious. When they invaded Canaan, they joined forces with the serfs who were under the heel of the Canaanite feudal lords. A Canaanite noble wrote to his Egyptian master for help: "Dagantakala to the King. Asks for rescue from the Habiru (an ancient name for the Hebrews). Let my lord protect his land from the hand of the Habiru. If not, let the king, my lord, send his chariots to fetch us, lest our own servants smite us."

"It's the truth," Aliza says, with a strange hardness. Tired out from her chores—with the end of school, she has been working in the communal laundry, sorting clothes for the washing machines—she yawns.

Without firing a shot, the Border Police scared off a band of Syrian infiltrators in the orchard last night. They were apparently trying to blow up the water pump. This morning, Cohen shows me the Czech pistol one of them dropped in a panic while making a run for the frontier less than 400 meters away. It's a 7.65 mm M1950, with an eight-round removable-box magazine that is inserted in the grip. He carries it around in his hip pocket while we work laying plastic irrigation pipes between the trees.

"There were three of them," he says. "You can see

their tracks, over here, in the mud. One of them slipped. That's the mark of his knee. *Verflucten Idioten!* It's hard to say which is worse. The wogs" —he says "vogs"—"or the pigs."

He shows me a scarred tree trunk raked by the tusks of a wild boar that regularly comes down from the Syrian mountains for apples.

"This tree's been ripped open twice already this summer. And there's nothing I can do to prevent it. I can't shoot them because we're too close to the border, and the bloody UN's liable to kick up a row."

"Have you ever lived in England?" I ask him.

"Yes," he laughs. "How did you know?"

"From the way you speak English."

"I was in the British army during the war."

"Whereabouts?"

"Africa, Sicily, Italy, and then France. I joined up right after I left Germany in '39 and was demobed in '45. I could have become a British citizen if I'd wanted to, but I came out here instead."

"How come?"

"I'd had it with the English up to here. Bloody anti-Semites, the lot of them. As bad as the Germans, in their way. A goy is a goy. Not that I took any of their guff, mind you. Not me. It's the first thing I learned. You've got to stand up to them. Show them that a ruddy Jew isn't afraid."

The clank, squeak, and roar of tanks, tonight, on the orchard road; light French AMX's used by the Israeli army. By the time Marilyn and I are in bed and have turned off the light, the metallic rumble subsides.

No work for me today. A blister on my right hand has opened and become infected. In the infirmary, where Esther smears it with an antibiotic ointment and bandages it up, I run into Edith Cohen. She has stopped by to pick up some tranquilizers for Miriam.

"It's American Librium," she explains, "under an Israeli trade name. I give her 10 milligrams, three times a day. Only a palliative, but under the circumstances, better than nothing. Poor thing. She comes to me and cries—with the tears streaming down her cheeks—because she can't stop overeating. But at the same time, she's terrified of losing weight—that enormous tummy, in particular—because it would reveal her developing breasts. At least that's what a psychiatrist in Haifa tells me. He says she overidentifies with her father, for one thing, and . . . All I know for sure is that for the last three years, ever since the beginning of puberty, she's been a very sick girl who needs professional help. Last night, she had another one of those nightmares about the Arabs who forced her to strip naked at the point of a knife and then mutilated her. Horrible.

"This morning I had another talk with her parents about psychotherapy. Actually with her mother. Hans wouldn't listen. He said he had a lot of work to do in the south orchard and walked out. Not that Lisel was more receptive. 'A psychiatrist?' she said. 'What for? It's only a phase. It'll pass.'

"Do you know her? Very, very German, as organized and meticulous as can be, and as cold as ice. Utterly indifferent to Miriam, even when she was a baby. Of course, she was in Theresienstadt during the war, where she lost her whole family, and that may have something to do with it. On the other hand, the girl desperately needs help. I don't know what to do."

When we see Miriam at lunch, she is stuffing herself with mashed potatoes. Seated beside her, at the head of the table, her mother has already finished eating and is reading a letter. She is an older, much thinner, and more attractive version of her daughter, with the same turned-up nose and blond hair, cut very short, that has just begun to fade and turn gray.

Marilyn goes off to help Aliza in the laundry.

At loose ends for the afternoon, I kill an hour or so in the dusty kibbutz office—a wooden shack near our room—where Seymour works as treasurer. Seated behind a metal desk, piled with papers and open loose-leaf ledgers, he is carefully checking the monthly accounts.

"A mess, as usual," he tells me, with a sigh.

He explains that since the members had no capital of their own when they founded the settlement, they borrowed the money from the government at 3½ percent interest, to be paid back over a period of thirty-five years. Additional short-term loans cost anywhere from 5 to 16 percent. Ten percent of the living expenses of the kibbutz each year goes for interest on various loans.

"Money is very tight in this country," he says, "and we're a lousy risk. Thanks to the cotton fields and the orchards, we managed to break even last year for the first time. But in my opinion, that's the best we'll ever be able to do. Most of our land is barely arable, and even with hired labor, we haven't got half the people we need to farm it properly. We're not likely to get them either.

"The government supports us because, in principle, it's ideologically committed to the kibbutz as a social ideal and because we perform an important defensive function on the frontier. But economically, we're a bust. An unpleasant fact, but the truth."

He returns to his papers, resting his cheek on his fist. On his muscular arm, covered with black hair, an American eagle is tattooed, holding a bunch of arrows in a claw.

"Do you know anything about accounting?" he asks, without looking up.

"No."

"Life is very strange. My father, who was a pants-presser in Chicago, wanted me to be a CPA. I have a knack for numbers. This was in Chicago, during the Depression, when things were very bad. His health was terrible—he had diabetes—and sometimes we didn't have enough money to eat, but he always managed to scrape up something to keep me in school. Only instead of being grateful, I resented it." He glances at me with an embarrassed smile.

"When the war broke out, I ran away from home and enlisted in the merchant marine. An education, believe me, in more ways than one. Some of the seamen were old Wobblies. I used to listen to them talk at night, and they lent me books. I was reading Veblen the night we were torpedoed off the coast of Ireland.

"After the war, my father still wanted me to become a CPA, and I went to night school for a couple of semesters. But my heart wasn't in it. When the Haganah asked for seamen to volunteer to smuggle refugees from Italy into Palestine, I jumped at the chance. Then the war broke out here, and I stayed. I joined the kibbutz in 1949." He laughs, in his booming voice. "And what do I do here? Accounting!"

I've just read a newspaper—the *Jerusalem Post*—for the first time in several days: two more incursions by infiltrators, one near Beth Guvrin, close to the Jordanian border, where a reservoir was blown up, and the day after that, at Kibbutz Iftah, on the Lebanese frontier, where a house was completely demolished.

The heat. I stretch out in the shade of the lilac bush behind our room, where Rama has dug herself a shallow hole in the red earth. She licks the sweat from my hand and sniffs at my bandage. Uri joins us at three, fresh from a shower, with a towel wrapped around his neck. The dog feebly wags her tail and then goes back to sleep with a sigh.

"Do you like it here?" he asks me.

"Very much."

"Where are you from? New York?"

I nod.

"I have an uncle there, in the Bronx. He's invited me to visit him whenever I like. I'd like to go sometime."

"You'd enjoy it."

"Have you ever been to Paris?"

"Yes."

"I'd like to go there too. When I was in school, I studied French and was pretty good at it. It's a beautiful language. Can you speak it?"

"Not a word."

"It's very expressive, like English, with a lot of synonyms. Not at all like Hebrew. In a way, Hebrew is very limited, especially in technical terms."

"That's to be expected, I suppose."

"I'd love to travel. When I was a kid, my father once took me on a trip to Beirut. I was too young to remember, but I understand it's a very sophisticated town."

"So I hear."

"Not like Tel Aviv. Tel Aviv is very provincial, don't you think? And so is Jerusalem, or Haifa. The whole country, as a matter of fact."

"I don't know about that."

"You're being polite. I wouldn't want to live anywhere else, you understand, but objectively, this is a very provincial place."

I look at him in astonishment and amusement, while he wipes his already sweaty face with a towel. As a Sabra, he has no feelings of Jewish inferiority, but is plagued, instead, by a sense of inadequacy as an Israeli.

"When I was a kid," he says, "people used to take vacations in the Lebanese mountains. It's cool there all summer long. The summers here are impossible. You never get used to them. I read somewhere, once, that the heat is easier for you to take than for people like me who were born here. You have more water in your tissues. Ours are all dehydrated. At least, it feels like it. Come on, Rama, I'll get you a drink. You don't look so good, either," he tells me.

"I've got the runs."

"Go and lie down."

When Marilyn returns to the room, she falls down on her cot and immediately goes to sleep. It's impossible for me to sit still. We are in the grip of another sudden *khamsin*, or heat wave. The gusts of hot, dry wind again seem to be blowing from the sun itself, as if it were breathing on the earth.

Today, Cohen takes me to the south orchard to see his favorite apple tree, which has consistently produced the best fruit. He gently pulls an apple from a branch, quarters it with his penknife, and after licking the blade, offers me a piece.

"Something marvelous, isn't it?"

"Delicious," I tell him.

"That's what it is. A 'Delicious.' Have some more."

"Thanks."

He watches me chew. "*Probieren geht über studieren*, eh? 'The proof of the pudding' . . . Fifteen years ago, when we planted our first trees here, all the experts said we were wasting our time. The soil wasn't deep enough, the climate wasn't right. No one had ever grown apples in this latitude before. But we went ahead and did it anyway. And now our yields and the quality of our fruit are equal to any in the world.

"Not that it's been easy. During the picking season, from July to mid-September, we work a thirteen-hour day, seven days a week. And the rest of the year, it's always something else. Planting, grafting, spraying, irrigation. We get our water from the Hatsbani, one of the sources of the Jordan. The best water in the whole country. This year I decided to install plastic and aluminum piping. It's much easier to handle. We have twenty thousand trees, and each and every one must be watered once every twelve days without fail. Quite a job, as you can imagine. But worth it. You'd be astonished at the extra growth. Still, it keeps me pretty busy, with not much time left over for anything else. It's been rough on Lisel and the kid, but they understand. This kind of life demands sacrifices."

At five, I go to the communal laundry shack, near the generator, to pick up Marilyn, whose stomach is also on the blink.

In the confined space, under the corrugated iron roof, the heat is overwhelming, despite the two huge electric fans set in the windows. There are perhaps eight women in the place, sorting out dirty laundry, operating the automatic washing machines, the gas driers, and an old-fashioned white porcelain mangle through which piles of damp bed linen are pressed.

Aliza and Marilyn are in a corner, ironing shirts.

"Tired?"

"A little," says Marilyn.

"You run along," Aliza tells her. "I'll finish up. There are only a couple more to do."

"No, I don't mind. Give me the blue one."

"It's a perfectly awful job," says Aliza. "Boring and exhausting. But you know something? I'd rather work here than teach."

"Why?" I ask.

"Because it seems somehow less bourgeois."

"She's special," says Marilyn, when we're alone in our room. "Most of the other women hate working in the laundry with a passion. I know, I listened to them grumble all day long. But Aliza's a special case. Kibbutz life gratifies her deepest needs. That's why she's happy here. And why a utopian ideal like this has such limited appeal."

A shot from the direction of the dining hall, just as we are about to go to sleep. By the time I have slipped on a pair of shorts and run outside, Uri is already there, carrying a rifle, which he evidently keeps in his room. Rama is barking. The moon is full. I can clearly see the dog's teeth gleaming in the pale light.

When we arrive at the dining hall and glance inside, through the double doors, Cohen comes out to greet us, grinning from ear to ear. Behind him, seated at a table, is Shlomo, with a pistol in his hand and a look of utter stupefaction on his face. The window to his left has been pierced.

"What happened?" I ask Cohen.

"He was field-stripping the Czech pistol."

"I could have blown my head off," Shlomo says. "The safety was off, and I didn't notice. Can you imagine that? After all these years?"

He is both chagrined and rattled—his face is pale —and to reassure himself, he examines the safety mechanism of the receiver, moving it up and down with his thumb.

"Can you imagine?" he repeats.

Another day off, this time because of my stomach, which has gotten worse. Esther thinks that Marilyn and I have picked up a bug, and has prescribed paragoric and a light diet. The very thought of food makes me want to vomit.

The sky is almost white, with a thick haze on the horizon above the Syrian mountains. Not a peep from the birds in the trees. Complete silence, except for the distant rumbling of a truck on the road and the dry rustling of leaves.

Taken with a cigarette, deeply inhaled, the paragoric gives me a cheap drunk. Perhaps I have a slight fever as well. When I return from a cold shower—the second in less than an hour—the gusts of hot wind, rebounding from the earth, dry my body underneath my thin cotton robe before I'm half way to the room.

Never have I felt so naked, nor derived such intense sexual pleasure from the sensation. But Marilyn is fast asleep. Another swig of the medicine knocks me out. I sleep through lunch and well into the afternoon.

By suppertime, we're both feeling better and can swallow a hard-boiled egg, a slice of bread and jam, and a cup of tea. We eat with Aaron Stern, with whom I'm very anxious to talk. When I tell him what Marilyn said about the limited appeal of the kibbutz, he puts down his dish of sardines, hesitates for a moment, and then slowly nods his head.

"She's right. What we have here, essentially, is a very special minority, with very special needs, living a very special k-kind of life completely different from the society around us. An extravagance, really, in this day and age. Oh, at one time, and not so very long ago, we performed an economic function—reclaiming land that no one else would settle. But, by and large, Israel has almost solved its agricultural problems. Apart from defending the frontier, we're of little practical value, I'm afraid."

Aliza, who has been listening, begins to interrupt him, but he goes on.

"Yet I think the k-kibbutz can still serve a purpose. Israel is becoming a normal industrial society with all of the drawbacks: urbanization, rootlessness, growing c-class differentiation, and an enormous immigrant problem as well. The k-kibbutz ideal of social justice is bound to have some influence in a country as small as ours. Don't ask me how. That's what we must find out, and one of the reasons I want to study and then work away from here. The important thing is not to isolate ourselves, but to increase our c-contacts with the rest of the world. Who can say what will result?"

The broken window pane has already been repaired. All day long, Shlomo has taken a merciless ribbing from everyone, to which he reacts with a good-natured, shame-faced grin that transforms his sharp features and makes him appear ten years younger, in spite of his thinning hair.

In his room tonight, it's evident that he has complete possession of himself again, or rather, that the skill of his hands, with those blunt fingers, has repossessed him. As we all sit around, listening to von Karajan's version of Mozart's *Fortieth Symphony* on the tape recorder, he replaces a plug on an electric cord, using his thumbnail to separate the conductors.

Only Aliza is ill at ease. Her thin, triangular face, with its beautiful eyes, is drawn about the mouth, and every few minutes she restlessly stands up, and finally goes outside for a breath of fresh air. The heat wave has broken, and a cool breeze is blowing from the east.

"I hate them. God, how I hate guns," she says, as we leave. "Why does he have to fool with guns?"

Ruthie and a group of her friends who are to be bar-mitzvahed spent today on their own in Haifa. As part of their initiation into adult society, they were required to ride the public transportation system up the Carmel, have lunch in a restaurant, make a phone call, and buy an inexpensive article of clothing.

It was the first time in their lives that any of them had ever handled money.

The girl is enchanted by the experience—she bought a little dacron and cotton blouse—but laughingly reports that one of the boys returned empty-handed because he mistook the size (42) of a T-shirt for the price and was too flustered to ask the salesgirl for help.

"It's not funny," says Shlomo, on the lawn after supper. "It's pathetic. We're afraid, terrified of exposing our kids to a different way of life for fear they'll be lured away."

Always the pragmatist, he insists that the kibbutz should stand or fall on its own merits, in active competition with the rest of Israeli society.

"Naive idealism is useless to us . . ."

How many times, now, have I heard him speak

that way? What is he thinking of? Seated beside him, Aliza squeezes his hand. When he gets up and goes back to their room, she smiles.

"A practical idealist," she says. "Very rare. But then he's different from most of us here. Have you noticed that? He's not escaping from anything like Aaron or Hans or myself. He accepts his past. Whatever it imposed on him. It's not really a personal need that makes him live on a kibbutz, but what he believes his country requires. An example of a just society based on manual labor. Not that he'd ever put it like that himself. At one time he desperately wanted to become an architect, but he gave it up to join the Palmach. After that, he felt that coming up here to defend the frontier and reclaim the land was more important than any personal ambition. And he's never regretted it. No matter what happens, I don't think he ever will."

At midnight, the light is still on in the museum where, for the second night in a row, Amos is at work. Streaked with dust, the window is almost opaque, and only a dim figure can be seen moving about inside.

Unable to sleep, I join him. He is arranging a new exhibit in a glass case: some barbed Mesolithic fishhooks, carved from bone, and a pendant, with a hole drilled neatly through the top, made from the canine tooth of a fox.

He has the true scientist's passion for categorizing

—but to what end? According to him, everything he collects is evidence of an essentially meaningless pattern: the endless repetition of similar events that extend from the remotest times to the present.

"Time is indivisible," he says. "Prehistory and history are all of a piece. I'm never so aware of it as when I'm working here, alone, at night. Just look around you. Three hundred thousand years, or more, at a single glance. And it's all one. Human needs or human psychology haven't changed. We've become more technologically proficient, that's all. Tractors instead of flint sickles, machine guns instead of spears. But neither the kibbutz nor the re-establishment of the Jewish state have any more objective significance than the Mesolithic occupation of the Hula, where I found those fish-hooks, or the Crusades."

He wipes the glass case with a damp rag.

Back to work in the orchard this morning, where Chaim and I lay aluminum pipes between the trees.

Instead of a skullcap, he wears a battered green fedora, with a greasy band, cocked over one eye.

He proudly tells me that with the money he and his wife will save this year, they will buy an air-conditioning unit for their four-room flat in Kiriat Shemona. They already own a radio and an electric refrigerator, for which they have learned to buy meat when it's cheap and freeze it.

"There you have it," says Cohen at lunch. "He's not only religious, but a born bourgeois as well, with all of your bloody middle-class aspirations. It's a pity. We could use types like that on the kibbutz."

"Have you ever asked him to join?"

"Years ago, we used to talk about it, but it never came to anything. His wife wouldn't hear of it. Their women, you know, are the real reactionaries. But if it comes to that, Chaim's an exception anyhow. By and large, they're a very primitive lot. I had an old man here, last year, to help with the picking, who insisted on kissing my hand when I gave him a lift back to town in the GMC. There was nothing I could do to stop him. He grabbed me before I even knew what was happening. Just for taking him home. What can you expect from a lot like that?"

After work, he invites me back to his room. On the wall, over the bed, is a large, framed photograph of himself in a British army uniform, with his arms crossed on his chest and sergeant-major's stripes on his sleeve.

"That was taken in Cairo, right after I was promoted. Lisel?" he calls out. "She's not here. Probably still at work. Well, sit down and make yourself at home. What would you like? Coffee? How about some fruit? I manage to nick some from the orchard now and again. Try a pear. They're ripe. Good, eh? That's a Bartlett. When Lisel gets back, we'll have some coffee.

"We come from the same town, you know, in Germany. Düsseldorf. We knew each other quite well before the war. Only my parents got out, just in time, and hers didn't. They were all packed off to Theresienstadt. Her parents died of typhus, and Lisel caught it, but somehow managed to survive. She was about to be transported to Auschwitz when they were liberated. She never talks much about it. There was a pit there, you know, where the guards forced Jews to beat each other to death with sticks. Preferably members of the same family. Brothers, or father and sons. Once in a while, although very rarely, they would refuse, and both would be shot on the spot. But most of the time, they'd fight. People will do anything to stay alive. You can't blame them, but it's disgusting, just the same. I often think about that pit. *Das Loch*, or *die Höhle*, we say in German, or better yet, *das Freigehege*, for animals. It was what the whole of Europe became for the Jews. And what England, or the States, could become.

"You don't think so? We won't argue. But take my word for it, goyim are the same everywhere. After I was promoted—in the field, mind you, as the result of an action—my lieutenant said to the captain, knowing damn well that I could overhear: 'Well, one thing you have to say for Hitler, sir, he has the right idea about the Jews.' I made up my mind to shoot him the next time we were out on night patrol. As it happened, a German mine did the job for me. Blew off both of his legs.

"After the war, I couldn't stand England, or the bloody English, with their red faces and watery blue eyes. A joke, eh? With my looks. In a way, that was the worst of it. With my face, I could have passed as an Aryan if I had wanted to. By that time, my parents were both dead. There was nothing to hold me in London. I had to get out and be among my own kind. It was almost a physical necessity, if you understand me, this craving for solidarity with my own kind.

"So, I made certain contacts, went back to Italy, where I joined the underground smuggling refugees into Palestine, and at last came here in 1947, where I discovered, quite by accident, that Lisel was alive and in training to join this kibbutz.

"Now listen to this. This is the odd part. She doesn't feel the way I do at all. Her experience in Theresienstadt left her not so much with hatred for the Germans, or the Gentiles in general, but with a kind of sneaking admiration for their efficiency and ruthlessness. How do you explain that? Jews, in the mass, depress her. A crowd in Tel Aviv, clamoring to get on a bus or into a movie, fills her with disgust. She likes it here because we are so isolated, and . . . But here she is, at last. Coffee, *Liebchen*, strong and black. We were just talking about you."

"So I heard."

"It's late," I tell them. "I ought to be going."

"Nonsense. A good strong cup of coffee first."

"Hans is a sentimentalist," she says. "At heart, only *ein guter deutscher Bürger*. In the camp, we were rapidly . . . *aus dem Irrtum gehielt . . . wie sagt man auf Englisch?*"

"Disabused," says her husband.

"Yes, disabused of such ideas about people. In the end, it was only the *unbeseelt* . . . you must excuse my English."

"The inanimate," says Hans.

"Yes, the inanimate, or the *unmenschlich . . .*"

"The inhuman."

"Yes, the inanimate or the inhuman things which remained to us . . . *Die natürliche Welt,* the physical world, because it was untouched, *unbeflecht,* unsoiled you say? by human beings . . . A little yellow *Schmetterling*, I remember, and a *Löwenzahn . . .*"

"A butterfly and a dandelion," her husband translates, as she goes on in German: "And so it is here, in the Galilee. The land alone, which absorbs me, a little more each year. Not that horrible orchard, or the wheatfield, but the uncultivated, worthless land that has been left alone. That land along the road to Horshat Tal, with those big black rocks. It would be nice to be buried there."

Marilyn and I accompany the eight children who are

to be bar-mitzvahed into Kiriat Shemona for an in-
terview with David Moreh, the Mayor.

He is an Iraqi Jew in his early forties, a dark,
handsome man, with heavy-lidded eyes, who studied
economics at the University of Baghdad and came to
Israel in 1949.

Kiriat Shemona, he tells us, has a population of
about seventeen thousand, of whom over 70 percent
come from North Africa, Iraq, Iran, and even India.
1952 to 1957 were the peak years of immigration.
The newcomers had to live in *marbarot*, sheds made
from sheets of corrugated tin, and there were not
enough jobs to go around. There was only seasonal
agricultural employment on the nearby kibbutzim,
most of which were loath to hire outside labor because of ideological principles. And the immigrants
themselves, who, for the most part, came from cities,
were unhappy doing physical labor.

In the last few years, the situation has somewhat
improved. The immigrants are provided with three-
room flats at nominal cost, and more of the kibbutzim
are hiring them. In addition, the government and
private investors have cooperated to build a cotton
thread factory just outside of town, with the hope
that the region will become a textile center.

In the meantime, the population still needs jobs.
Even with government subsidies, the average family,

with five children, has a monthly income of only one hundred and fifteen dollars.

As Moreh speaks, I have been taking notes. When I pause to turn a page and happen to glance up, I'm aware that his audience is restive and bored. Ruthie, who is sitting next to me, idly sketches little birds on the margin of her notebook. The boy next to her, slumped down in his chair, with his legs stretched out, is staring at the ceiling through half-closed eyes. It is not so much rudeness that prompts their behavior but incomprehension. The experience of those destitute immigrants to Israel in the last ten years who now form over half the population of the country is unimaginable to them.

In the dining hall, after Friday evening meal, Nat tells me that he's asked the Saba to teach the eight bar-mitzvah children a portion of the Haftorah for the ceremony next week.

"It's a small portion of the Book of Samuel. He was delighted to do it, but insisted that the boys wear yarmulkas when they study, like a bunch of yeshiva students. Some of the members protested that I've included traditional religious elements in the ceremony, but I think it's a good idea. Not because I believe," he adds quickly. "Nothing like that. I come from a good socialist home where I was brought up as an atheist as a matter of course. And I still am. But

I'm also a history teacher who knows that religion has been the sum and substance of Jewish civilization for almost five thousand years. You can't ignore that. It's what defined and preserved us all throughout the Dispersion. A commitment to adhere to the Law, to the morality of the Torah, no matter what. 'Justice, justice . . .' Remember? Can you recall how the Holy Yehudi interpreted that? What has socialism given us to match those words of an obscure eighteenth-century rabbi who lived in a Polish ghetto? What? Marx's 'moral futurism'? That whatever will inevitably happen in history is, for that very reason, and that alone, just and right? Is that what I'm supposed to teach my kids?"

On the way back to his room, he suddenly adds, "I won't do it. We're still Jews, you see, and that heritage is—or should be—part of us and our children. But it's useless, I suppose. What can I hope to accomplish by having them memorize a prayer to a God in whom I have never believed myself? How can they possibly learn to appreciate the moral values of a civilization while rejecting the faith from which they're derived?"

"How did you?"

"Yes, that's strange, isn't it? But then, all my passions are intellectual." Seated, silently, in front of his bookcase, with his legs crossed, he furiously strokes his mustache as if to calm himself.

"And yet," he says, "when all is said and done, Wolfe was right, you know. At Lod, I mean. He did the right thing. If it had been up to me, I would have botched it."

Marilyn and I spend the Sabbath morning swimming and sunning ourselves at Horshat Tal. The flies draw blood. But the grove is jammed with children from nearby kibbutzim, soldiers with a few hours' pass, whose units are stationed along the frontier, and a crowd of Moroccans over from Kiriat Shemona for the day.

There are perhaps twenty or thirty of them— men, women, and children—camped under the huge oaks on the far side of the pool where an enormous swan, with clipped wings and scarlet feet, glides across the water. Was the bird here before? If so, I never noticed it. Once in a while, it raises itself up, with a straightened neck, and beats its crippled wings in the air. The Moroccans feed it bits of bread.

They are picnicking on sandwiches, oranges, peanuts, and beer. A bottle shatters on a stone. Their loud, cheerful voices—yelling in Arabic and Hebrew —fill the air, and before long we hear Arab music— the throb of ceramic drums and a squeaky violin.

We walk over. The pock-marked fiddler, wearing dark glasses, is blind. The women squat in a circle, clapping their hands, dressed in cheap, bright print dresses, all red, yellow, and blue, with gold necklaces and spangled bracelets that flash in the sun. With their high, swollen stomachs and sagging breasts, they are all old before their time. Even the children have aged faces; the pinched features and dry complexions of old men. Only the men in their twenties appear to be their true age. Dark-skinned and mustached, with long, dirty fingernails, three of them begin to dance. And then only one is left, wearing a sleazy nylon shirt, unbuttoned to the waist. His hairless chest gleams from sweat.

"It's a belly dance," Marilyn whispers.

And so it is. With his hands locked behind his neck and a grin on his face, he slowly rotates his torso, and then his hips, at a barefoot woman cracking peanut shells with her teeth. She shrieks with laughter, a hand at her throat. Arched over backwards, his arms at his side, the dancer thrusts his quivering thighs in her face. His eyes are closed, and his tongue protrudes between his lips.

The music gets faster—one phrase, in a minor key, repeated again and again—and suddenly he wheels around and smiles at a young soldier in uniform with his sleeves rolled up and a Belgian FN slung over one shoulder. The woman shrieks again, even louder, and then lets out a whoop—a quavering Indian war whoop, from a western movie, but without using her hand. How is it done? By vibrating her tongue? She whoops again.

The soldier smiles and says something in Arabic, low and distinct. Where did he learn it? In school? He is obviously a Sabra of European descent—the son of Russians, perhaps, with the wide face, high cheekbones, snub nose, and the straight blond hair of a Slav. He speaks Arabic once more, a few words out of the side of his mouth, and the dancer, the woman, and the fiddler laugh. One of the drummers, who holds his drum, shaped like an hourglass, under his left arm, abruptly switches rhythm and sings out the words of a new song in a high, nasal voice. Pausing only an instant, the fiddler follows his lead, and while everyone sings aloud—even the soldier, who throws back his head—the dancer moves toward him, gliding sideways, with one shoulder raised. He repeats the same gestures as before, in a frenzy of excitement, shaking his shoulders, while he rotates his stomach and then his hips, all the while gazing into the soldier's eyes. He laughs hoarsely and turns away.

"So you sensed it, did you?" Amos asks me when we return to the kibbutz for lunch. "Well, it's not as preposterous as it might seem. Nor as unusual. These groves and high places, like some other archaeological sites in the country—the caves at Carmel, for instance, or Masada—have you ever climbed Masada? —seem in some way to have retained their own time.

They're so much a part of the distant past, so saturated with it, they appear to have preserved it intact.

"At Horshat Tal, it's because of the sunlight, I
think, filtering through the leaves; that greenish light
and the play of the shadows on the ground. And the
water, and the flies. Even the acorns scattered on the
grass. It's a real forest glade, left over from the time
when most of the Galilee was covered with trees. An
anachronism, and you can sense it. Very strange. It
gives me the same feeling.

"And if those Moroccans of yours seemed to belong there, it's because they do. Psychologically,
they're not very different from the primitive Israelites
who danced under those trees three thousand years
ago. Nor, from what you tell me, have the dances
changed very much, either. Although homosexuality
was punishable by death, according to Mosaic law, it
remained a problem for generations after the conquest of Canaan.

" 'There shall be no harlot of the daughters of Israel, neither shall there be sodomites of the sons.' The
Bible was talking about the ritual prostitution of both
sexes. The Canaanites practiced it in places like
Horshat Tal, and the Jews were forever sneaking off
to those sanctuaries for a bit of fun."

On the way back to our room, we stop off with
Amos at the museum for a few minutes.

"Three summers ago," he says, "one of the Moroccans who worked in the orchard wandered in here one afternoon, and I showed him around. When he saw that basalt mortar and pestle on the shelf, his eyes lit up. He wanted to buy it for his wife to make flour. I tried to explain to him that it was Mesolithic —thousands and thousands of years old. 'That's impossible,' he said. His wife had a smaller one like it at home. She had made it herself in Rabat, only eight or nine years ago. 'Well, this one is thousands of years old,' I kept repeating like an idiot. He looked at me as if I were crazy or trying to pull his leg. I couldn't make him understand.

"The passage of all those centuries had no meaning for him. And why should it? His material culture —that basalt mortar—has, to a large extent, remained the same. Children think much the same way, but for different reasons. Perhaps because the historical sense is learned, the result of a specific education. Last year, Seymour's youngest kid was astonished to find out that you could telephone Jerusalem. He said his teacher had told him that the city had been completely destroyed by the Romans. And not only children. Did you know that Aristotle believed that the Trojan wars were contemporaneous with him? That's a fact. It's hard for us to grasp, but true. The Greeks had no conception of a lineal chronological progression. History, as we understand it, was invented by the Hebrews, and for ideological considerations. The Prophets, who believed that it had meaning: a beginning, a middle, and an end. And thanks to the modern historicists, like Marx, we suffer from the same illusion."

"You're not a socialist?"

"Of course I am. And a Zionist too. Absurd, isn't it? But one doesn't believe in something because it's true, but because it's good."

Back to work in the orchard this morning, thinning trees. I've become fairly adept at it, going only for those branches, laden with inferior fruit, that hang downward, almost touching the ground. Cohen is always a little ahead of me, working to my right. Neither of us speaks.

I'm beginning to understand what Stern means when he says that physical labor is the religion of the kibbutz. It's a rite, requiring all my concentration and energy. Almost every movement is rigorously prescribed, and there are moments when I experience what a devout Catholic must feel while celebrating Mass—a peace that subdues the intellect.

But only moments. The rest of the time, my mind wanders erratically, and I'm bored. Or, actually, so tired that I think of nothing at all, except a cold drink of water.

And Cohen? He works steadily, with a slight frown, even when the rest of us knock off for lunch:

delicious scrambled eggs again and strong tea. Half an hour later, when he finally joins us, he sits down beside me.

"Well, that's it," he says. "All finished. We've done a good job. Now there's almost nothing to do until the picking. That's the real work. Twelve, thirteen hours a day, and then sleep. You've never slept so well in your whole life. Like a log. Like the dead. Are you a good sleeper? I slept badly for years until I took this job. Now I have no trouble. I snore. Poor Lisel raises hell, but it doesn't make any difference. Nothing wakes me up, especially after a day of picking. I tell you, it's something wonderful. Wonderful," he repeats.

So that's it. For him, this is a soporific.

The Saba is feeling better. Late in the afternoon, I watch him fix a sandal. He works in front of his repair shop, seated on a low, wooden cobbler's bench, with the last between his legs, putting on a new sole. He has already removed the old one and now sands the bottom of the sandal and one side of a fresh piece of leather to make the two pieces rough and easier to cement together. Once they have been glued, he holds the sandal in his left hand, close to his chest, and, with a curved knife, cuts away the excess leather to make a perfect fit. Finally, slipping the sandal on the last, he carefully punches holes in the new sole with an awl and sews the sole to the sandal with a long steel needle and heavy thread, using the blunt end of the awl to push the needle through.

"He's content," says Nat at supper. "In spite of everything, just living here is enough for him. He believes that this country is holy and that it was given to the Jews for accepting the burden of the Torah and making a covenant with God. The Exile, to him, is a punishment for breaking the Law. It'll end with the coming of the Messiah. In the meantime he waits, satisfied that he has a little taste, right now, of what will eventually come to all of us. It's a curious paradox, when you come to think of it. If he really believes that history has a divine purpose, that man alone can't 'force its end,' so to speak, and redeem himself, then the old man should logically repudiate everything that Zionism has achieved. But he doesn't. Maybe his faith isn't strong enough. Maybe he doubts, and doesn't admit it to himself."

"Why have all the beaks been cut?" I ask the Chink in English. As I don't know the words in Hebrew, I point to one of the chickens in a wire cage and make a snipping movement with my fingers.

"Ah, the beaks," he says in English. "Yes, if not, they peck out their eyes."

We're in one of the poultry houses, hosing down the concrete floor. Flies, the stench of chicken shit, and disinfectant. When we talk, we have to shout because of the incessant cackling of the birds—over eight thousand Rhode Island layers.

David, who's in charge of the whole business, yells at the Chink in rapid Hebrew that I'm unable to follow.

"*Nu?*"

"I forgot," the Chink tells him.

"He forgot to change the wet litter in the brooder," David explains to me in English. "I told him to do it yesterday. If any of those chicks catches bronchitis, I'll break his ass."

"Where'd you learn your English?" I ask him.

"At school, under the British, and then when I was a liaison officer with the UN observers at OP 1. There was a Swede and a Dutchman with me, and English was our common language. I saw the Dutchman again last night." He brushes a fly from his face. "We had a little trouble."

"What happened?"

"The Border Police shot three Syrian infiltrators near here, at Kfar Yuval."

"What time was this?"

"About three-thirty in the morning. I got a call about four to come and inspect the bodies. They were regular Syrian soldiers, or certainly trained and equipped by the Syrian army, with khaki uniforms, sneakers, hand grenades, Karl Gustaf submachine guns, and two antivehicular land mines. Mark Fives. I suppose they intended to plant them in a field and blow up a tractor."

Edith Cohen is all excited tonight. Her twenty-year-old daughter, Elana, who is finishing up her two-year hitch in the army at GHQ in Tel Aviv, has just phoned to tell her that beginning the day after tomorrow she has wangled a four-day pass and will be coming home.

"She's a wonderful kid. I don't know what I would have done without her when Moshe died. That's him. The charcoal drawing on the table. Elana did it about three years ago."

"She's very talented," says Marilyn.

"And doesn't she know it! She wants to be an illustrator. Books, things like that. She's been studying since the age of fourteen at one of the big kibbutzim nearby where they have art classes twice a week.

"That's Moshe, exactly. Getting fat, but still handsome, and so proud of that thick head of hair. The wave in front, over the forehead. She captured it exactly, and the expression in his eyes. He wasn't feeling too well at the time. He had a bad heart. Rheumatic fever as a child. The doctors told him it would be a miracle if he lived until forty. He made it, but three years later, a year ago next month, on the twentieth—" she snaps her fingers, "—just like that, without any warning, on the path, coming back to the room after supper. We expected it, but I don't have to tell you, it didn't make it any easier.

"I don't think I fully appreciated what living on a kibbutz meant until then. It's indescribable. The genuine, really genuine, warmth and sympathy for everyone. Even people you hated, or hadn't spoken to for years. It was like being part of some huge, fantastically closely knit family. No. Even more than that. Much more. I can't begin to describe it . . .

"Moshe was originally a Czech, from Prague, who was lucky enough to escape the day before the Nazis marched in. He managed to get to New York, and we met at a Zionist rally near Union Square. Just one of those things. We had seats next to each other and got to talking. He had been in the country just a couple of months, five or six at the most, but he already spoke English perfectly. He had a great talent for languages. After that, one thing led to another, and we got married.

"It wasn't easy. Jobs were hard to find. He did everything. Worked as a lathe operator, an electrician. When the war broke out, he was frantic. He tried to enlist, but no one would have him. He even took a correspondence course and trained himself as a radio man in hopes of joining the merchant marine. But with his bad heart it was no go. He was bitterly disappointed and wound up working in the Brooklyn navy yard as a welder. We made up our minds to come out here right after the war and join a kibbutz. I was always a Zionist and a socialist. I suppose I got it from my father. He was an immigrant from Odessa who never really made it in the States. He owned a candy store on Eastern Parkway in Brooklyn, and with four kids it was a real struggle to stay alive. He sent us all to college, though. CCNY. Anyway, he was always a socialist and, with the rise of Hitler, a Zionist as well. As far as Moshe was concerned . . . Have you got a moment? I'll read you one of his letters . . . This was written on a boat coming here in 1945. He went on ahead to clear the way. You can copy it down if you like.

" 'I still think,' " she reads aloud, " 'that the kibbutz is a way of life best suited to us first and foremost because of the social security that it gives you, because if I die I know that somebody will worry about you and because I will be able to live productively in the time that's left to me without worrying about food, doctor's fees, and other little details. Although maybe you don't realize it, more than half my life has passed . . .' "

"Moshe?" says Aliza. "He was someone special. Not only because of his kindness or sense of humor, but his competence. My God, how the man worked! We all pleaded with him to take it easy because of his heart, but he wouldn't listen. He said it was a matter of time, anyway, and he wanted to accomplish something. He did. Have you seen the cooperative cold-storage plant for apples we have in Kiriat Shemona? Just beyond the town, on the right-hand side of the road, going toward Tiberias. The big building, you can't miss it. It's the biggest and most modern cold-storage plant for fruit in the whole country. Eleven kibbutzim in this area own it. We desperately needed one. It's what makes our orchard so profitable. You can preserve the fruit and then sell it, at the best price, any time of the year.

"Anyway, Moshe and Hans studied up on the thing, became experts, helped design it, and then Moshe ran it—the whole business—for three or four years. That was in addition to being in charge of our power plant here.

"I was in Tel Aviv the day he died. Shlomo sent me a telegram, and I came home immediately. The funeral was the next morning. It was horribly hot. He was the first member of the kibbutz to die, and I don't think any of us actually realized what was happening. We didn't even have a cemetery. Finally we decided to make a little plot in the field on the other side of the orchard road. The funeral was very simple. A couple of the members, Hans and David, said a few words over the open grave, and that was it—just what a fine person he had been and how much he had meant to all of us. He didn't want any kind of service; as a matter of fact, he had left written instructions. No rabbi or even Psalm reading, anything like that. It was what Edith wanted too. Nobody says kaddish for him, except the Saba. It makes Edith angry, but he does it anyway."

Because of the trouble at Kfar Yuval, the Border Police, wearing their green berets, have already been here twice tonight—once after supper, in the dining hall, to confer with David, the military commander of the kibbutz, and then again on their rounds in a jeep, at about one-thirty, across the field parallel to the frontier on the other side of the orchard road, where they stop for a few minutes and turn off their headlights. Because of the waning moon, it's appreciably darker than even a few nights ago. The jeep is barely visible.

Marilyn and I have remained awake with Edith, who is on night watch in the children's houses. It's a duty required of all the women here about once a month and consists of little more than checking each house every hour or so to make sure everything is all right. We begin in the infants' house, filled with high chairs and cribs, where all the kibbutz babies are taken to live about six weeks after they are born. Here, day and night, the mothers come to feed them, but, in addition, there is a trained nurse on duty, always the same woman, who remains with the babies all day long.

"It works out rather well," Edith tells us, folding a pile of diapers and putting them away on a shelf. "The babies, of course, never confuse the nurse with their mothers, from whom they get their love, or neuroses, as the case may be. On the other hand, there's always an expert around to give advice, if the mothers will accept it. But you'd be surprised at the know-it-alls, some of the intellectuals, particularly, who refuse to listen. It's their privilege, I suppose, but if the baby's really in trouble, the nurse tries to do what she can. Provide a little tender loving care, mostly, which some of the mothers, for one reason or another, seem unable to do. But like everywhere else, the mother-child relationship is the crucial one."

We move on to the kindergarten house, where the children live from three and a half or four years old until they are six.

"There's room in here for about twenty kids, with four in each room," says Edith. "This is obviously the kitchen, with this little dining room attached; that's the classroom, and there, at the end of the hall, is the isolation ward, for contagious diseases. How about a glass of milk? There ought to be some in the fridge."

"No thanks."

"Each group has its own nurse. It's curious. Have you met Tamar? She's absolutely superb, gentle and understanding as could be, but mildly manic depressive. That's the wrong word. Moody, if you know what I mean, with a lot of ups and downs. Nothing serious. But almost all the kids who've had her seem to exhibit the same personality pattern. It disappears after a few years, but it's still noticeable while it lasts."

She shines her flashlight into the room on my left, where a woman with dark, braided hair is sleeping in a bed next to a cot where a little boy is lying with his face to the wall and his feet uncovered.

"That's Shula with Amnon," Edith whispers.

"His mother?" Marilyn asks.

"Yes. He's four, at the Oedipal stage, when the kids often wake up in the middle of the night and cry. We have an intercom, by the way, that Shlomo installed, which picks up all the noises in the children's houses so the night watch can hear everything that goes on and be anywhere in a few minutes. But for some of the kids at this age that isn't enough, so we allow their mothers to sleep in the same room with them. It's fairly common. Occasionally, on my advice, a kid will be allowed to sleep in his parents' room for a while, and they'll come and eat with him here. The food is much better than in the dining hall, by the way. I'm dying for a smoke. How about it?" she asks me. "I've got some Pall Malls."

"Love one, if you can spare it."

We go outside and sit on the steps.

"Do you know," she says, "that after all these years, smoking these damn things still makes me feel guilty. A bourgeois indulgence that I ought to be able to do without, but I can't."

When she finishes her cigarette, she stands up. "You wait here. I'm going to check on Miriam."

She walks down the path, throwing the beam of her flashlight straight ahead of her until it illuminates the stucco wall of the building where the teenage group lives. It's like all the others: a single-story bungalow with a sloping tile roof. Edith goes inside. The flashlight shines through one window, and then another, while we wait.

"Asleep, thank God," she tells us, with a smile, when she returns. "She's always had trouble sleeping. When she lived here, in the children's house, and woke up screaming for her mother, Lisel wouldn't come. She said it was a matter of principle."

Marilyn and I return to our room where she has arranged a bowl of daisies on the table.

"No," she says, unbuttoning her blouse. "I wouldn't want to bring up my kids that way. It's too organized, not spontaneous enough."

She examines her bare legs covered by mosquito bites and gets into bed. A naked light bulb on the porch remains burning and I can still make out her

features which always, unexpectedly, remind me of
my own.

"It's nonsense," she says. "Life can't be contained
by any ideology. It's too complex, too diverse to be
. . . What in heaven's name are you doing?"

"I've got a bite on my backside the size of a half-
dollar."

"Scratch it."

"That's what I'm doing."

"Better?"

"A little."

"Then come and kiss the back of my neck," she
says.

Aliza and Marilyn have spent part of the afternoon in
Kiriat Shemona buying surprise presents for Ruthie's
Bar Mitzvah on Saturday: a red dress from her parents and a little leatherette toilet kit from us, with a
pocket mirror, scissors, a metal nail file, a comb and
brush, and a tiny vial of perfume.

I'm collecting eggs in a heavy wire basket. Five times
a day, as soon as they are laid, I bring them to David,
who washes them in a rubber bucket.

About five years ago, he tells me, some of the
members here seriously considered having the Chink
expelled from the kibbutz for laziness and general
incompetence. It finally came to a general meeting, at

which neither he nor his wife was present, where the whole thing was thrashed out.

"I thought about it, but finally voted to let him stay," David says. "He's good for nothing, but what about his wife and kid? We have some responsibility toward them. We couldn't just throw them out to starve. They would have, too. The son of a bitch couldn't earn a living anywhere if he tried. Shlomo agreed. There was a big fight, but we finally brought the rest around . . . Where is he, anyhow? Go and tell him to come in here and help me pack these, will you? We send them to Haifa this afternoon."

After supper, Edith introduces us to her daughter, Elana, who arrived on the six-o'clock bus from Tel Aviv. She's a very pretty, rather plump girl, with her father's dark, wavy hair and her mother's command of English, which she speaks with a guttural Sabra accent. For a while we chat in the dining hall, over tea, and then Edith insists on inviting us all back to her room.

"Boring, boring, boring," the girl says. "I sit all day typing up stupid orders or getting tea for the *Seren*, the captain, who's married and has three kids but can't keep his hands off me." She laughs. "Last week when he got fresh I spilled a glass of tea on his lap. Not boiling, but hot enough to cool him off, for a while, anyway. If I get a pass in the evenings, I generally go to a movie, or have an ice cream at one of the cafés on Dizengoff. The crowds are incredible, absolutely incredible. You wouldn't believe the numbers of people just walking up and down. Awful."

"Have you done any drawing?" her mother asks.

"A little, but not much. The barracks are jammed, and it's impossible to find a place to be alone, even if you have the time. I've done a few sketches, portraits of the girls, in pen and ink. Nothing special. And a couple of bad illustrations from an Agnon story, 'In the Heart of the Seas.' Have you read it? It's about some Hasidim who makes a pilgrimage here in the middle ages. I could hardly make head or tail out of it. He's a mystic, and his Hebrew is terribly difficult. Anyway, I did them with a brush and india ink. And I also bought some more Chinese white, imported from Germany and very expensive, but marvelous."

"Ink?"

"Yes. Oils or even water colors don't tempt me at all. I'm a draftsman, if anything. It's the line that counts." She makes a graceful, sweeping curve in the air with her forefinger. "How're things here?"

"Fine," her mother answers.

"Where's Uri? I didn't see him at supper."

"I forgot to tell you. He sends his regards. He had to drive in to Haifa overnight for some supplies."

"Oh?"

"He told me to tell you he'll be back early tomorrow morning."

"They've been seeing each other for about four months," Marilyn tells me when we have returned to our room.

"How do you know?"

"Edith told me. She thinks he's a nice boy, but she's worried that they're sleeping together."

Today Aliza takes us to visit an acquaintance of hers, Laura, a social worker, who works with immigrant children in Kiriat Shemona. She is a member of Kfar Szold, a nearby kibbutz down the road on the Syrian frontier.

"I hardly know her at all," Aliza tells us, on the way over in the car. "We occasionally meet on the bus into town and talk about our kids. She has a lovely daughter. When I happened to mention last week that you were an American writer who was interested in Kiriat Shemona, she absolutely insisted that you come over for a chat."

The tall, stoop-shouldered woman is waiting for us outside her room and invites us inside. She graciously serves us coffee and little squares of chocolate. I eat three without thinking, and then, at a glance from Marilyn, restrain myself. Chocolate is very expensive in Israel, and from the look of the shabby little room it's obvious that this kibbutz spends very little money on its members' personal comfort. We're actually in a wooden shack. Despite the heat, there are no ventilators on the windows.

"Every morning, when I leave here to go to work," she says, in English with a German accent, "I feel as if I'm going abroad to a different country. No, not only that. But into a different time. The distant past. And no one, either on the kibbutzim or in the big cities, appreciates the problems of these new immigrant towns. I would estimate that over eighty thousand immigrants have passed through Kiriat Shemona in the last ten years, unable to adjust themselves to the conditions. At least eighty thousand. But when I once mentioned this figure to Shazar, the President of Israel, he simply refused to believe it.

"The whole thing was badly planned from the beginning," she continues. "The location, for instance. Distribution is a terrible problem. The road, over the mountains to Haifa, the nearest big city, is totally inadequate for the amount of traffic needed to supply the town. Nobody does anything about it.

"But that's nothing. These people need jobs, jobs more than anything else, and there are simply not enough to go around. Most of them are on some form of relief."

Fanning herself with a newspaper, Laura tells us that she was originally a German refugee who fled to Holland, where she was hidden in a Christian home throughout the war. "At enormous risk to their own lives, every minute of the day and night, for years, without one word of complaint or reproach. They said it was their Christian duty. I have never met people who were so compassionate. If I had a religious temperament—the slightest inclination—I would have converted and become a Christian myself."

When she resumes talking about Kiriat Shemona, she leans forward in her chair and her voice quavers with agitation. "The immigrants there are the dregs. What we call in Hebrew 'the desert generation'— those in the Bible who were condemned to wander in the wilderness and die without ever entering the Promised Land. Only here they are. Good for nothing, except, perhaps, their children, or their children's children. North Africans, Indians, Eastern Europeans. It makes no difference. The dregs," she repeats. "We even have some Hungarian procurers, with their prostitutes. Gangsters . . . The Persians are the most primitive. You wouldn't believe how primitive the Persians are."

She takes a thick bundle of manila folders from the bookshelf and opens one.

"Here's an example for you. A Persian mother who burned her eight-year-old daughter's genitals with a hot iron because she was jealous of her husband's attention to the girl. In this instance, the woman was psychotic, but brutality like that, toward children, and incest, is quite common among them. And, as far as I can tell, without any manifestations of guilt. None whatsoever. A father rapes his daughter or breaks his son's fingers, one by one, and, when confronted by the police, shrugs.

"Sometimes I feel that these people are not so much primitive as degenerate, from centuries of being debased by the Muslims. They can't adjust to modern life. They become depressive, or violent.

"In Morocco, or Persia, the father is the undisputed master of the family; his word is law. Here, the children go to school or pick up new ideas on the street, and they refuse to obey. The men feel castrated. Sixty percent of them do make-work, like planting trees, which further lowers their self-esteem because any kind of manual labor is degrading to them. They say that the Europeans on kibbutzim who work the land must be mad. A Turk told me that on a kibbutz, where the men work so hard, without getting paid, there must be free love. Some special form of compensation.

"There's almost nothing we can do for them. When they break down, psychotherapy is useless because the cultural differences are too great. We can only administer drugs to keep them calm. I would estimate that one-half of the population of Kiriat Shemona is on tranquilizers of some kind, or antidepressants. One-half! And we haven't even got a trained psychiatric nurse in town to make sure they take the medicine regularly or get the proper dosage."

She leafs through the papers in another folder.

"The children are caught between two worlds. Torn apart . . . This file is about Masouda, a fourteen-year-old Moroccan girl, whose parents have been here twelve years but can't speak a word of Hebrew. A decent family life, eight children, all very close, because they're deeply religious. The girl is intelligent. When she finished elementary school, her teachers and I recommended that she attend a technical high school in town. Her father protested. He didn't want his daughter to get a secular education. We finally persuaded him.

"In the last year, she's become very ill. A congenital heart condition. Her father blames it all on me and the school. She needs an immediate operation to save her life, but he won't allow it. 'If she dies,' he says, 'it's God's will.' We're in the process of getting legal permission to go ahead without his consent, but you can see the problem. We've undermined the old man's authority and, as he fears, the faith of his daughter. Masouda is very submissive, but she has already begun, very tentatively, to ask me questions about the Bible. 'Who married Cain?' Things like that, which I try to avoid answering. After all, it was religion that preserved her people's identity for thousands of years and brought her family here. But now it threatens her existence. And later—what will happen later on?"

On the way back, Aliza says nothing until we cross the little bridge that spans the Banias, another headwater of the Jordan that rises in the Syrian heights.

"As I said, we always talk about our kids. I don't know why, but it never crossed my mind to ask her about her work. You know how it is. It's impossible to believe, but I've lived here for almost twenty years and never heard the facts about Kiriat Shemona until today . . . Half the town on tranquilizers, and the kibbutz does almost nothing to help. Nothing, except hire a few workers and send a bundle of old clothes there a couple of times a year . . ."

The general meeting, at which Stern's future will be decided, is tonight. We gather in the dining hall, after dinner, facing Seymour, who, as elected managing secretary of the kibbutz, will conduct the proceedings. Beside him, at another table, Uri is sitting, studying notes on a pad.

By nine, we are ready to begin. The air is already thick with cigarette smoke. I rapidly count heads. Only forty-six out of the ninety members of the kibbutz have bothered to attend. Aliza whispers that the turn-out is surprisingly good. Many meetings have only ten or twenty members.

Stern and his red-haired, freckled wife, who looks Irish, with her fair complexion and green eyes, are sitting in the rear, near the back door. She is knitting a sleeve of a blue sweater. His face is perfectly impassive, until he suddenly glances up and smiles.

A tiny sparrow has somehow become trapped in the hall. It flies from one rafter to another, to a window, where it thumps against the glass, fluttering its wings, and finally to a rafter again, in one corner of the ceiling at the far end of the room, near the kitchen, where it remains, twittering, and, with a flick of its tail, lets one go—a white drop—that spatters on a freshly washed floor. In spite of the amused laughter, coughs, scraping of chairs, and subdued murmur of voices, which continues throughout, the meeting has already begun.

Uri has been rapidly reading the minutes of the last meeting, and when he has finished Seymour informs us that all security measures are still strictly in force until further notice. He speaks Hebrew with an atrocious Chicago accent.

Now he clears his throat. "Well, you all know the issue," he says in his booming voice, and very briefly, nervously plucking at the black hair on his arm, tells us that he's in favor of allowing Aaron to leave the kibbutz for two years to study at Rehovoth.

"He's done a superb job in the cotton fields for five years. As treasurer, I ought to know what that's meant to the economy of the kibbutz. And, with Uri here to continue the work—he knows almost as much about cotton as Stern—there won't be any trouble. Furthermore, in the long run, Stern's studies will probably help us improve the crop. Certainly the marketing."

But for some reason, perhaps to gather his thoughts, he abruptly stops for an instant, and in the brief pause a woman seated to my right, at the next table, speaks out. It's Shula, who, a few nights ago, was sleeping in the children's house with her son. Her dark, braided hair, coiled doubly around the crown of her head, has a reddish gleam in the light.

"No," she says quietly. "He'll be studying agricultural management in general, and when he's finished he'll be spending most of his time away from the kibbutz. We won't benefit at all, at least not directly. The kibbutz will be losing a very capable worker for good. And we simply can't afford it. We haven't enough manpower as it is. I say no. Definitely not."

She is loudly supported by another woman, whose name I don't know, with a thin face and red nose. "I have nothing against Aaron personally. You all know that. But it's a question of principle, and that's all. Our ideal is a small, homogeneous, socialist community, based on agriculture, which . . ."

Aliza, who has been translating the rapid Hebrew discussion, leans closer and whispers in English, "Aviva. She works with me in the laundry. Three years ago, she wanted permission to go and study to be a teacher. Geography, I think. I can't remember. Anyway, we had enough teachers, so she was refused permission. Now, when anyone else wants a leave of absence to study anything . . ."

The discussion continues, while the sparrow flutters from one rafter to another and then back again to the corner. David, one of Stern's best friends, gets up to speak, but so softly that it's almost impossible to hear him.

"I know that Aaron deserves to go." From under his bushy eyebrows, he glances at Stern, who smiles at him, momentarily closing his eyes, with a nod. "If any of us deserves to get what he wants, he does. No one has done more." Another glance at Stern, who encourages him with a smile. "But I can't agree. I'm against it. We can't afford to indulge ourselves. The needs of the community come first, and Shula is right. What we need are more manual workers, not intellectuals, who . . . We simply can't afford to lose him."

He sits down.

Finally it's Stern's turn. He rises. There is complete silence, except for the click of his wife's knitting

needles, which ceases when he draws a deep breath
to speak.

"Da-da-david is right, absolutely right. M-m-my
responsibility to this k-k-kibbutz comes first, before
. . ." Nervousness has made his stammer worse than I
have ever heard it, and he must periodically stop
talking altogether and hold his breath to force out
the next word. "B-b-but we're all different personali-
ties, with entirely d-d-different needs. I've finished
my job in the Hula, and now I'm stagnating there . . .
s-s-stagnating. No use to m-myself or to anyone. And
as I g-get older, Uri will be able to do a b-b-better job,
because he's young and has the strength. It's something we never face. G-getting older and losing our
strength. But I'm still young enough to s-study, and
prepare myself to be of some further use to the k-k-
kibbutz movement. P-perhaps even here. I don't
know. I c-can't promise that. But to be allowed to be
c-c-creative again is all I ask."

He sits down and wipes his moist lips and chin
with the back of his hand. His wife resumes knitting.
Seymour raps his knuckles on the table beside him,
calling for a vote.

"All in favor?"

Aliza and Shlomo raise their hands, along with
fifteen others. There are three against, including
David. For some reason, the other members abstain
from voting.

Marilyn and I help rearrange the tables and chairs, empty the tin ashtrays, and then go outside, where Aaron and David are talking. The crowd mills around, chatting, when Aviva suddenly points to the sky and exclaims, "A meteor!"

"No, you idiot. It's one of the American space satellites."

We follow the ball of light, moving in an arc against the stars, until it disappears behind the Syrian mountains.

"That's a very good one of Amos."

"You like it?" Elana asks me. "Have you noticed that the two halves of his face don't match? And not because of his bad eye but because of the bone structure, particularly the right cheek and lower jaw. The scarred half is much better looking. If you look carefully, nobody's face matches exactly. The halves are always different. In your case, it's quite obvious. Your left eye is much smaller than your right. The lid droops. But that's not all. Turn your head to the left. Oh yes, it's not only the eye. Your right profile is quite different. Subtly, but not at all the same."

We are in her mother's room this afternoon, going through the thick sheaf of pen-and-ink drawings that she has done over the past three years. They are all realistic portraits of members of the kibbutz or sketches of them at work, in the fields, the cowshed, poultry house, or orchard. She shows me one of Hans Cohen, half way up a ladder, thinning an apple tree. His face is hidden by his upraised arms, but from the set of his body, his broad shoulders, and short legs, it's unmistakably he.

"I did Daddy in charcoal," she says, "because it's softer and it was easier to express his gentleness that way, by the shading, and capture those shadows under his eyes. When he was tired—he was always tired—he had those terrible, brownish-blue shadows under his eyes. His fat cheeks made them more noticeable. Can you see the color? I used chalk. Look carefully. Wait, the light's reflecting on the glass. There. Just a smudge of blue and brown, and picked up here again, in the hair, and the shadow of the adam's apple. But for the rest, I've used pen and ink. I adore that wonderful deep black india ink against the white paper. Or just a carefully defined, pure black mass, like the shadow of that apple tree. Do you like Beardsley? I've learned a lot from him in the last little while. Simplicity, the sweeping line, and when to ignore perspective entirely, or distort it to make a dramatic point. He's dreadfully decadent, I know, a real bourgeois esthete, but by God he could draw. Look at this, for example, this sketch I made of Uri two years ago, with all the cross-hatching, all that unnecessary junk, and the one of Amos."

"What's all this in the blue folder?"

"Experiments. I did them six months ago."

"Can I see?"

"If you like."

"Who's he?"

"Elijah."

"Who?"

"The prophet Elijah."

"Standing in front of the dining hall?"

"Yes. Announcing the coming of the Messiah. Can you read Hebrew? It says at the bottom, 'Now peace will come upon the earth.' The legend is that three days before the Messiah comes Elijah will appear in *Eretz* and make that announcement."

"Who told you that?"

"Nat. One day in class, years ago, he was talking about those figures from the Bible who became part of Jewish folklore during the exile. I didn't pay much attention at the time, but almost a year ago I began to get tired of realism, just copying from life. I wanted to do something imaginative, fantastic, but Jewish, specifically Jewish."

"Why?"

"It's a long story, hard to explain. Anyway, I thought of Nat. We had a long talk, and I did these."

"Why hasn't Elijah got a face?"

"That doesn't work, does it? To tell the truth, I couldn't find a model, at least not on the kibbutz. The

Saba was sick at the time, and an old Moroccan worker in the orchard refused because he said I was giving him the evil eye, or something. Then I thought, according to the legend, Elijah's supposed to be an angel, and if I left his face a blank, a white blank, radiating those streaks of light—that's Chinese white—against the black wall of the dining hall, it might convey . . . It doesn't convey anything, although I think the figure is well drawn, the folds of the robe and the gnarled staff."

"Very well done."

"You really think so? I know it's very Beardsley-esque, but if I keep at it I'll develop a style of my own. I'm going to try, anyway. If I can find a model, I'm going to try Elijah again, too, maybe in front of the cowshed, with a calf in the background. It's a nice legend, his coming here." She laughs. "Of course, if he did, and made his announcement, nobody would listen."

I leaf through several pages of carefully articulated anatomical studies: the skull, sketched from all angles, the lower jawbone, drawn from below, the skeleton of the right arm, bent at the elbow, with the humerus, ulna, and radius labeled in English lettering, the pelvis, the left leg, and then a whole series of musculature. The right arm, again raised, and bent at the elbow, with the fingers spread, and the notation, in English, obviously copied from an anatomy book:

"Extensor Carpi Radialis. A musle [sic] which extends and abducts the wrist. (See pages 34-35)."

"This is only a preliminary study," says Elana. "I used a brush instead of a pen."

"It's astonishing. What is it?"

"Enoch becoming Metatron. 'And Enoch walked with God,' " she quotes the Bible in English, " 'And he was not; for God took him.' "

"Yes, I know."

"The legends say that he was transformed into Metatron, the highest angel. The Lord of the Face. The Angel of the Divine Presence. He became very important in kabbalistic mythology, particularly German thirteenth-century kabbalism, where he's the Scribe of the Heavenly Court, the Keeper of Heavenly Secrets, and the Great Mediator."

"Where did you learn all that?"

"From Nat, I told you. Fascinating, isn't it? He also gave me Ginzberg to read. *The Legends of the Jews.* It's beautiful. *Eze jaffe ma'od!*" she breaks ecstatically into Hebrew. "Listen to this."

She takes a paperback book from the pile on her mother's nighttable, opens to a page, marked by a little scrap of paper, and reads aloud, in English:

> When Enoch was transformed into Metatron, his body was turned into celestial fire, his flesh became flame, his veins fire, his bones glimmering coals, the light of his eyes heavenly brightness, his eyeballs

torches of fire, his hair a flaring blaze, all his limbs and organs burning sparks, and his frame a consuming fire.

She has chosen to portray him in the midst of being transformed, with his legs apart, his arms raised in agony, his head thrown back, and his hands covering his eyes. Streaks of white light shine from between his spread fingers, and his black hair is on fire. The lower part of his face is fleshless, a naked jawbone, connected to the spinal column. His legs and the left side of his body are fully fleshed, but, as though he is being flayed alive, the edges of the skin are ragged, revealing the musculature of his pelvis, his stomach, and his chest. That too has been torn away, showing his breastbone and the right half of his rib cage, which is on fire. The right arm has already been transformed into glowing coals. With extraordinary skill, she has preserved the skeletal structure—the humerus, ulna, and radius—but by composing them of irregularly shaped black lumps, delicately separated by dots of Chinese-white ink, the illusion is complete.

"What's this mean?" I ask.

"The cobbler's bench?"

I simply hadn't noticed it before; in front of the figure, between his legs just below his knees, is the black, one-dimensional silhouette of a cobbler's bench, with a last, on which is an inverted heavy work shoe, with one shoelace hanging down and the tip of the sole rolled back but connected to the bottom of the shoe by a diagonal thread.

"That's the most important thing of all," Elana tells me. "He was a cobbler. That's why he became Metatron."

"I don't understand."

"It's very complicated. He . . . Ask Nat, I can't explain it . . . It would make a wonderful painting, don't you think? The color of the fire. Blue and yellow, green, orange, and red. But I have no real feeling for it. Anyway, I think doing it in black and white, the burning I mean, is something of a *tour de force*, don't you?"

"Very much so."

"I'm glad you like it."

Another day in the poultry house, where David and I pack hundreds of eggs in cardboard cartons, each containing two rows of six eggs.

"Keep their large end up," he tells me. "That's the way. That preserves their normal balance. If you pack them right, you get fewer stuck yolks."

The din in the dining hall is terrific: hammering, sawing, the whine of an electric drill. Under Shlomo's direction a waist-high wooden stage, almost the width of the room and a quarter of its length, is being constructed for tomorrow's festivities. The frame is complete, and now the planks of the floor are being laid. Seymour's wife, Yora, a placid, motherly Sabra with a round face and huge breasts, is perched precariously on a ladder, stringing up a red curtain.

The drill again, and a shower of sawdust. Seated on top of another ladder, with a coil of wire looped over his shoulder, Shlomo is drilling a hole through a rafter for a spotlight. Two are already in place, with amber filters.

Shouts from the kitchen. Edith and her staff are frantically preparing four hundred cold chicken dinners for the members, their families, and friends from all over the country who have been invited to attend the ceremonies. Many will remain overnight, and places must be found for them to sleep. Aviva is in charge of making the arrangements. Her thin, pale face is buried in a mass of papers spread all over a table near the door. Aliza goes to tell her that she's expecting Shlomo's mother, sister, and brother-in-law.

After dinner, on the lawn, another crisis, but this time because of the Saba. With trembling lips, on the verge of tears, Rivka tells us the story. "He's impossible. An impossible, fanatic old man, who gets worse every day. I don't know what I'm going to do about him. Sometimes I think . . . He's not feeling well again, so I told him to stay in bed all day, and he promised he would if I came this afternoon, before sundown, and cooked his chicken for tomorrow, the damn Sabbath meal, so he wouldn't be responsible for having a daughter of his violate the Sabbath by lighting a fire in his house after dark. He was exhausted and slept all day. I was so busy in the kitchen—it's a madhouse—that I forgot. It completely slipped my mind. By the time I got to his room, it was already dark. The candles were lit, he had said his prayers, and was eating—a brisket he cooked last night. But there's nothing for him to eat all day tomorrow, except a herring, half a loaf of bread, and a piece of stale cheese. Nothing substantial, no chicken, or soup. And he needs it, to keep up his strength.

"What's the use? He won't touch any of our food, of course, because it's not kosher, contaminated. We don't keep separate plates for meat and dairy. '*Tref*,' he says. I pleaded with him, 'Let me cook the chicken anyhow. What's the difference? You know I don't believe in God.' Do you know what he did? He hit me, slapped me across the face, and called me a goy. On and on . . . I was ungrateful, nobody but Mama ever loved him or cared about him, his children wished he were dead . . . ranting and raving. I swear I thought he was going to have a stroke. His face turned purple.

" 'Ungrateful!' " Her tone is suddenly furious. "Do

you know that after Mama died I was the only one who agreed to look after him? Not Chana, his darling Chanele, his favorite. Oh no. She has a four-room apartment in Ramat Aviv—her husband is a bank clerk—but she wouldn't take in her sick father for love or money. She admits it. 'He's a *cvetch*,' she says. 'He upsets the whole house.' He and her husband 'fight all the time.' Her daughter 'needs a room all to herself.' 'Ungrateful!' . . ."

She bursts into a peculiar dry sobbing, like hiccups, gets up hurriedly, and runs off.

"He's old, so old, and terrified of death," Aliza says, after a pause. "Or maybe not death so much, but . . . Nat tells me that although he was glad to teach the kids the Haftorah for tomorrow, he refuses to come to the ceremony because it's not a genuine religious service. He says he's afraid to take a chance when he's so close to meeting his Maker."

As the light is still on in Nat's room, at a quarter after eleven, I drop in to chat about Elana. He puts down a book on Israel's wildflowers and rubs his bloodshot eyes. "I have no idea why she suddenly became so interested in the legends about Elijah and Enoch," he tells me, stifling a yawn. "A couple of years ago, in class, she was like all the others. Bored and contemptuous, fantastically contemptuous, whenever I talked about the culture of the Diaspora. For all the kids, it's a blank in Jewish history, a time to be ashamed of, when we never fought back. No, I don't understand it."

"Why was Enoch a cobbler?"

"Yes, she was particularly fascinated by that. Well, according to the Kabbalists, he not only sewed the sole to the shoe but with every stitch joined the upper and lower worlds. While he worked, you see, he prayed with such concentration, meditating on the significance of what he was doing, that he was able to draw them together. He . . . What he did, essentially, was to transform a profane action—ordinary work—into a sacred one. And in the end, he was transformed himself."

Another yawn, and again he covers his mouth with his hand.

"Nobody can say I haven't done my part. Ask anybody. I was in the Palmach for two years under the Mandate and during the war, in the Jerusalem sector, where it was plenty hot, believe me. But enough is enough, as I always say. Times have changed, and you have to change with them. That kind of idealism is dead, nobody takes it seriously any more, and besides the country is on its feet. You have to be realistic. These days it's every man for himself."

All this, in a steady stream, from Seth, Shlomo's brother-in-law, who works for a construction company in Tel Aviv. He speaks a rapid, slangy Hebrew, which Aliza must translate for me fast as she can. He's a tall, lanky Sabra, in his late thirties, who wears sideburns and combs his sparse hair forward to conceal a high, bald forehead.

We're outside, lying on a blanket spread on the grass. Shlomo is in the dining hall, making last-minute adjustments on the lights for tonight. His mother is lying down in his room with a headache from the long drive in the old Ford pickup truck that Seth has borrowed for the weekend. Seth's wife, Pnina, sits beside me, crosslegged, chewing a blade of grass. Her pinched nose, accentuated by her rimless glasses, makes her look like her brother, but she's taller.

It's a little after one. A warm day, with a particularly strong wind. The kibbutz is overrun by hundreds of guests, some of whom cluster in little groups on the lawn around their families or friends—the members who have invited them. The ceremony begins in about an hour. Ruthie, who has already been given her presents—an overnight bag from her aunt and uncle, cash from her grandmother—dashes by, with shining eyes and flushed cheeks. Overcome by shyness, blushing and stammering, she is hardly able to thank anyone.

All day long Adi has watched her with a jealous and superior air. The little toilet kit amused him enormously. Before his mother was able to stop him, he snatched the pocket mirror and was outside, flashing the refracted sunlight in the eyes of anyone coming up the path from the dining hall.

"Mama, I'll murder him!" his sister screamed.

Luckily, late yesterday afternoon, Marilyn and Aliza drove into Kiriat Shemona, where they bought him a big, brightly colored book about rockets and space exploration. Still, whenever he catches sight of his sister he smirks, and if his mother isn't watching sticks out his tongue.

The first ceremony of the day is held on the rise above the dining hall. By a quarter after two, we're seated at one end of a huge semicircle of tables—planks set together on sawhorses—heaped with food. The wind, at our backs, is blowing stronger than ever, mercifully keeping away the flies but occasionally knocking over a bottle of wine.

In the center of the semicircle, a small wooden platform has been built on which Seymour is standing. To his left, on the grass, the eight bar-mitzvah children are all lined up. The girls are wearing starched white, short-sleeved blouses and blue skirts, and the boys, open-necked white shirts and blue trousers.

Seymour raises his right arm for silence. But most of the huge crowd ignores the gesture. It takes almost half a minute until conversation dies away and he can begin his speech. But then all I can hear is the wind, the rustling of pine needles, and the squeak of a branch behind me. By some fluke, the wind blowing diagonally across the rise, from the southeast, carries his voice away from us, so that perhaps only half the crowd, or less, can actually hear him.

It's as if I were watching him from behind a thick pane of glass. He nods at the children, smiles, all the while moving his lips but not making a sound. Adi laughs, and his mother tweaks his ear. Applause from the other end of the semicircle. We all join in. Apparently he has finished.

Then, looking at the children, Seymour says something else—obviously the name of the first boy in line, who steps on the platform, shakes the man's hand, and is given a black book and a small rectangular box. The third boy, all arms and legs, stumbles on the way down, and to relieve the tension we laugh.

When the last girl leaves the platform, the crowd applauds again and begins to eat. Ruthie comes and sits down on the bench beside her mother, who kisses her on both cheeks. Her father hugs her. The book she has received is a Bible, the Old Testament, with her name printed in gold lettering on the leather cover. She opens the rectangular felt box and beams with pleasure. Inside is a steel wristwatch, with a heavy chrome band. We all congratulate her, and she blushes.

The dinner lasts an hour. As usual, there isn't

enough food: one cold, broiled quarter of a chicken per person and a spoonful, or two, of cold chopped liver with onions.

"To Ruthie. *Mazeltov!*"

We drink one round of toasts, from little plastic glasses filled with sweet Carmel wine. At the end, I notice, among all the litter—the paper plates, tin knives and forks—that almost all the wine bottles on the tables are still more than half full. Everyone has been drinking orange soda.

Shlomo elbows his way through the crowd to Seymour, shakes his hand, and solemnly congratulates him on his speech.

Mrs. Wolfe's headache has gotten worse. She's lying down again, in Shlomo's darkened room, with a handkerchief, soaked in vinegar, on her forehead. Outside, Ruthie is admiring her new watch, which looks enormous on her delicate wrist.

"Honestly?" she asks me. "But he has such a loud voice."

"Not a word. The wind was blowing the wrong way."

"That's too bad. You missed a wonderful speech."

"What'd he say?"

"He said that a Bar Mitzvah on a kibbutz is something very different and very special. It means that we've become adults, with adult responsibilities to the kibbutz and to *Eretz* to . . . to work together to build the country and lead socialist lives."

By eight in the evening the dining hall is so hot, so smoky and jammed, that Marilyn and I have stationed ourselves by the back door to be able to duck out occasionally for a breath of fresh air.

On the stage before us is a long table, covered by a dark green cloth and set with two tall, red, flickering candles in brass holders, with a bowl of daisies between them. The eight bar-mitzvah children are seated in a row behind it, bent over their open Bibles. The boys put on their yarmulkas, and with one high-pitched, ragged voice the children begin chanting in the traditional singsong of the Orthodox Jew at prayer.

" 'And Hannah prayed and said, my heart rejoiceth in the Lord, because I rejoice in thy salvation. There is none holy as the Lord; for there is none beside thee, neither is there any rock like our God.' "

Seated to my right, against the wall, Lisel has stood up, and making her way between the packed benches, to murmurs of annoyance, strides up the center aisle, past us, and out the door. But the children have obviously not noticed.

" 'Talk no more exceedingly proudly; let not arrogance come out of your mouth; for the Lord is a God of knowledge, and by him actions are weighed.' "

Then, suddenly, the big blond girl at the end of the table begins to giggle, infecting the boy next to her, who stops chanting, and with his hand over his mouth turns his face aside. One by one, the children break up, giggling, or laughing aloud, and at the same time desperately trying to regain control of themselves and resume the recitation.

" 'And they that were hungry ceased; so that the barren hath borne seven.' "

A fresh outburst of laughter. Ruthie bites her lower lip.

" 'The Lord killeth and maketh alive; he bringeth down to the grave and bringeth up.' " Amnon, David's son, chants on alone. Ruthie joins him, followed by the dark-haired boy to her right, until, finally, all the children are again caught up in the rhythm of the biblical Hebrew and finish the selection.

The entire audience, which has been maintaining an embarrassed silence, as though holding its breath, heaves an audible sigh of relief. Everyone begins talking at once.

Marilyn and I go outside for a while. Elana and Uri stroll by, arm in arm, on the way to his room. When we return the adults are performing, and the audience, particularly the kibbutz members, are intermittently convulsed by laughter. Shlomo, Yora,

Seymour, Amos, Edith, and Aviva are putting on a skit based on the characters in *Winnie the Pooh*.

Breakfast with Aliza, who asks me if I saw Lisel leave the dining hall during the ceremony last night. "I can't blame her," she says, slowly stirring a spoonful of sugar into her mug of tea. "And yet, when Nat proposed that the children read from the Bible in the traditional way, as if they were actually praying in a synagogue, I voted for it. And for some reason, I'd do it again."

In the poultry house David hands me a shovel. I shovel chicken shit from the brimming dropping pits beneath the cages into a wheelbarrow, which the Chink wheels away.

"What's the significance of the cobbler's bench?" I ask Elana in the dining hall after dinner. She glances impatiently toward the door, where Uri is waiting for her.

"Didn't you speak with Nat?"

"Yes, but what does it mean to you? You said it was very important."

"It is," she says. "But it's hard to put into words. I suppose it was the ideas about work that struck me: that it can become sacred and completely transform you."

"But Enoch became an angel. The concept is specifically religious."

"Not for me, it isn't. I don't believe in God. Religion has nothing to do with it. But the ideas are still very beautiful and still have some significance for us. Or at least they did for my father. He worked himself to death, but he believed that it was worth it. He once told me that his work here . . . He once said that before he came to the kibbutz, he was a *Luftmensch* with no real purpose in life, but that his work here changed all of that. It gave his life meaning, and that changed him."

"How?"

She hesitates. "Well, for one thing, he said he stopped biting his nails."

Uri signals her, by raising his head, but preoccupied with her thoughts she ignores him.

I'm completely bushed. David finishes cleaning out the dropping pit, and I watch him go at it, effortlessly lifting shovelful after shovelful, in a steady, unbroken rhythm. Only the veins standing out on his sunburned neck betray the slightest strain.

"You're out of shape," he tells me.

"You know it."

"You ought to see my kid put in a day's work. He helped out here last week, packing the eggs and then loading cartons in a truck. Five hours straight, without a break, except to get a drink of water or take a leak. He's skinny, but strong as hell for his age. Not that he's stupid. Far from it. You saw him the other night. That kid's got *sechel*. You know. Brains."

"Presence of mind."

"That's the English expression! Exactly. But he's not one of your intellectuals, by God."

"I can believe it."

With Elana again, in her mother's room. Before returning to duty in Tel Aviv, she's been going through her portfolio of drawings and is unable to decide whether or not to throw away her "Elijah."

"I'll keep it," she says finally. "The composition's not too bad. Originally I'd intended to do two more as part of a set illustrating the legend. It says that he'll appear three times in *Eretz* before the coming of the Messiah. There are a lot of things I'd like to do along those lines."

"All on Jewish themes?"

"Jewish, Israeli . . . You can't completely separate the two cultures. They're different, of course, but one comes from the other and it's impossible to escape from the past. And why should you? Tradition is important . . . Yes, I'll keep it," she repeats. "The composition's good. You notice the way the tree emphasizes the vertical staff?"

"Did she really say that about tradition?" Nat asks. "But then she's someone special. An artist. As for the others . . . You saw how the kids reacted to the Bar Mitzvah. It meant nothing to them because they've been taught that what we've created here is something entirely new, a complete break from our religious heritage. Which it is. But what we've really done is secularize it; we've denied God in his own name. Redemption, the sanctity of work, the return of the exiles, the creation of a just society: these are essentially religious ideas. But we've found no adequate way of expressing them."

Midnight. An explosion rattles the windows in our room. With Rama whimpering at our heels, we run to the dining hall, where a small crowd has already gathered, waiting to hear from the night watch or Border Police, who, after half an hour, come to report that infiltrators have set off a charge in the orchard. Because of the darkness—there's no moon—they have been unable to determine the extent of the damage. Tomorrow morning someone will have to go down and check the water pump.

Another explosion during breakfast, at exactly eight-ten, which shakes the whole dining hall, knocking my mug of tea on the floor. At the next table, Esther bows her head over a plate of fried eggs and sliced cucumbers. David sneezes. A clatter of plates from the kitchen, but not another sound until we hear the roar of a jeep, the screech of its brakes, and Avram, one of the boys who works in the orchard, bursts into the room.

"Esther . . ."

"Yes, I'm coming," she tells him, but for a moment more she remains where she is, without raising her head.

Twenty minutes later, the boy returns alone.

"It's Seymour," he says. "On the orchard road. His tractor went over a mine that the Syrians must have planted last night. He's still alive, but his leg . . . His right leg is all twisted back, with the foot under the armpit. Esther did what she could until the ambulance came, but I don't know."

At ten I join Shlomo at the crater, almost ten feet deep, in which the tractor, a big red John Deere, has been sheared into three parts. The engine is split in half, and the upended rear points at the sky.

"It was a 'sandwich,'" he explains. "Fifteen kilos of dynamite. Two plastic mines of 7 kilos each, with a kilo brick of the stuff in between. The water pump, by the way, is undamaged. They obviously set off the charge in the orchard as a lure."

Noon, and no word from Safed. Cohen tells us that when they heard the explosion and ran to the road, they found Seymour fully conscious but in terrible pain.

"Not from his leg, oddly enough, but from his

right hand. The middle finger was smashed. We all stood around, gaping at him like a bunch of idiots, absolutely paralyzed, until Chaim pushed me aside and jumped into the hole to hold his head and wipe his face with a handkerchief. Yora came down with Avram. She even remembered to bring a couple of bed spreads from the laundry to wrap him up in case of shock. Except for his hand, there was hardly any blood. Esther said that the leg was burned, and that seared the wound closed. She bandaged him up and gave him a shot of morphine, but it didn't do much good. He kept moaning, 'My hand. My hand . . .' "

At 9 P.M. Esther returns to the kibbutz for the night. "It's still touch and go," she says. "They had him on the operating table for five hours and almost lost him twice. They had to amputate part of his finger and his right leg above the knee. When the doctor told Yora, she said she was so grateful he was alive she didn't care. It was a miracle he didn't die on the way to the hospital. He was conscious the whole time and in agony from his leg, pleading for more morphine. I didn't know what to do. The danger of shock was acute, but finally I decided to take a chance and give him another shot. It was a mistake. Just after we passed Rosh Pinna, he suddenly clamped his teeth together and said, 'I can't breathe.' And he stopped. I managed to pry open his jaws with the handle of a scalpel and give him mouth-to-mouth resuscitation. About a minute before we reached the hospital, he started breathing again. Yora was yelling at him all the time, at the top of her lungs. 'Breathe, Seymour. For God's sake, breathe.' The driver complained about the noise. He said that the road was dangerous enough as it was and all the commotion made him nervous."

"Will Seymour die?" Adi asks his mother, as she puts him to bed.
    "He might."
    "Is there going to be a war?"
    "I don't know."
    "I hope so."
    "Why?"
    "So we can kill all the Arabs, and there'll be peace."

Cohen reports this morning that Chaim spent all of last night in a Moroccan synagogue in Kiriat Shemona, praying for Seymour's recovery.
    "It seems that Seymour met him on the road and offered him a lift down to the orchard on the tractor, but he preferred to walk. Just one of those things . . ."

"Horrible. It's horrible," Aliza whispers at lunch. For an instant, I have the impression that she's referring to her food, a plate of burned stew swimming in brown grease, which she has left untouched. But obviously it's the waiting that has shattered her nerves, along with the cessation of almost all conversation, which persists now at every meal.

News, at last. At 10 P.M., Edith returns from the hospital.

"He'll live, but he's in excruciating pain from his leg. The doctors are afraid to give him any more morphine, so they've decided to inject pure alcohol into the raw stump to deaden the nerves. At least that's what I think they're using. The trouble is there's none in Safed, or the hospital in Tiberias, so they have to refine some themselves, in the lab, which will take another twenty-four hours."

Shlomo and Amos are on watch, while Marilyn and I have a cup of coffee, with Aliza, in her room. I go outside for a smoke. Once again, in the moonless night, the mountains surrounding us have been obliterated and the lights of the Syrian positions on the slopes above us burn in empty space beneath the stars. The armed men stroll by, talking with David. Then they turn right, at the end of the path, and disappear into the dark.

June: 1967

Dear Hugh and Marilyn,

What fun to know that Switzerland is nice, in spite of the bad weather. Maybe it'll clear up in Geneva.

I'm sitting quietly in the room listening to a concert on the radio—Brahm's Fourth. Everything has happened so suddenly that we're still all in a state of shock. One by one, almost all the men have disappeared, because they've been called up, and the kibbutz has been left almost alone to us women. Of course we too are on the front and have to prepare for war, as incredible as it seems. God help us, I can see no other way out, and the thought is almost unbearable. I must say, though, that we're not despondent and the mood is generally good. We're so busy that we really have no time to think.

To add to it all, Shlomo had an unexpected appendix attack on Friday and was in the hospital for a few days. They said they would eventually have to take it out in three or four months. He came home today feeling reasonably well, but I've hardly seen him. To be honest, I didn't know whether to be pleased or not. What, after all, is safer—to have a comparatively minor operation or every night to be laying mines right under the Syrian guns?

The children—all the children are wonderful and seem to understand that they must behave themselves.

How wonderful it would be if you could come. Maybe, Please God, this will prove another false alarm and you can come just for fun.

Much love to you both from everyone,

As ever,
Aliza

June 9. Is the dog dead? A small, black, shaggy mutt, with yellow eyes, lies in the corner of the restaurant, in front of the pickle barrel, impervious to the Israeli artillery barrage. No, his ears twitch, but only when I offer him a French-fried potato does he rise to his stumpy legs. The fourteen-year-old girl who has been serving me stands in the doorway of the restaurant to watch another helicopter bring down the dead and wounded from the slopes of the Syrian mountains to the hospital here in Safed.

When I look outside, I can see nothing. The barrage, obviously raking the Syrian emplacements, seems to double in intensity, but the guns are completely concealed. Their firing echoes and re-echoes in the narrow street, between the low stone houses. An old Romanian couple—there's something in the woman's wrinkled face that vaguely resembles the girl's in the restaurant—sit on folding chairs in the sun. We are on the highest plateau in the country, and the air is cool.

More and more artillery. I run to the main street, Jerusalem Road, where I have parked my car. It's a little red Volkswagen, rented from Hertz last night, when I arrived in the country on the first plane out from Zurich. But it has no radio. All I know is that all the Israeli settlements along the Syrian frontier have been under intensive artillery bombardment since Monday, and that sometime early this morning Israeli troops and tanks began the assault of the Syrian heights. All day long I have crawled behind military convoys going north: open trucks and buses, ordinary civilian buses filled with troops, huge 300 hp Mack tank carriers transporting British Centurions or Super-Shermans—American Sherman tanks refitted by the Israelis with thicker armor, diesel engines, and 100 mm guns.

Six, eight, ten more rounds. "155's," says the bored MP in the middle of the street.

"How can you tell?"

"Training. You have to train your ear to . . ." But it's at least the fourth time this afternoon that I've tried to engage him in friendly conversation, and he breaks off, shaking his head.

"Orders are orders," he tells me again. "The direct road north from here to Kiriat Shemona is closed to all civilian traffic."

"But I've been stuck here for almost three hours."

"Listen to me. Find a decent hotel, the Herzia, for example, take a shower, have supper, and go to bed early. By tomorrow morning, the chances are you'll be able to get through."

He's a sergeant, with a splendid black mustache, who happens to speak English perfectly, although with a slight, indefinable European accent.

"What about the long route?" I ask him.

"What do you mean?"

I've been studying a tourist map. "Suppose I go back to Meron, north to the Lebanese frontier road, then head east until I connect with the main road north again?"

"Along the Lebanese frontier?"

"Why not? There's been no fighting up there, has there?"

"Be careful," he yells, as I start the car.

"I will."

"The road is lousy. You'll have to hurry if you want to make Kiriat Shemona before dark."

He's right. Most of the frontier road is a single, un-paved track strewn with stones. But I drive as fast as I can. The swollen sun is setting. Occasionally, irre-sistibly, I glance down the steep slopes to my left at the Lebanese villages—neat, stone houses with red tile roofs. A huge carob tree, to which a cow is teth-ered, spreads its lengthening shade. Not a glimpse of a human being.

Then, a burst of light ahead of me, where explo-sion after explosion detonates on the slopes of the Syrian mountains. The car rattles over the stones; I can hear nothing, but the flashes of orange fire and white, gray, and black smoke make me stop. A faint booming. Another orange explosion, and simultane-ously, perhaps two hundred yards away from the first, another, and then a pause, and a hundred yards north of that—although it's hard to estimate the distance from here another. Further up the slope, a curious, almost perfect ring of flame that continues to burn, giving off clouds of white smoke.

I see—or think I see—the reflection of the setting sun on a plane as it banks to the east.

Dusk. Kiriat Shemona is completely blacked out. The road is lined by troop carriers, half-tracks, Super-Shermans, and Centurions heading for the front. At the junction just north of town, a few kilometers from the kibbutz, the MP refuses to let me pass.

"Listen to me a minute," I tell him in Hebrew.

"Do you speak English?"

"Yes."

"Then fuck off."

He waves on a Centurion and a self-propelled French 105. I pull off the road, turn off my headlights, and wait in the dark. The MP has a flashlight with a red lens. He shines it in my eyes.

"You don't understand English?"

I drive back to the police station in Kiriat Shemona.

"It's no use trying to get through tonight," says the officer in charge. "The kibbutzim are still being shelled. Stay here. I'll take you to a hotel where you can get something to eat and some sleep. Believe me, it's the best idea."

Behind him, across the room, a Moroccan cop is thumbtacking a "wanted" poster to the bulletin board. The criminal's face is primitively drawn. Except for his remarkably prominent ears, he could be almost anyone.

The hotel is about a kilometer away, on the other side of the main road. The windows have been painted blue. Inside, two flickering candles illuminate a few tables, chairs, and a refrigerated display case in which there are some bottles of milk and beer. The owner is an unshaven old man, with white whiskers, who wears a yarmulka. Tonight is the beginning of the Sabbath. All he has for me to eat is a warmed-up half of a boiled chicken, cold mashed potatoes, and green beans.

". . . When they first came they were animals. But a few years in *Eretz*, a little education, and you'd be surprised . . ."

I'm astonished to discover that the old man is talking to me in Yiddish, which I can hardly understand, about the non-European immigrants to Kiriat Shemona.

"Have you got a beer?" I ask him.

"One beer. Certainly."

The fatty, yellow skin of the chicken, with its pimply feather follicles, has suddenly made me violently nauseated.

"Never mind the beer," I tell him. "Where's my room?"

It's a cabin, sparse but immaculate, with two beds, a shower, and a clean towel hanging on the bathroom door. As soon as I'm alone, I go outside on the wet grass in my bare feet. It's a cold night. The traffic on the road has ceased, and except for the cicadas, which fall silent when I approach, it's perfectly still. Spread out to the east above me are the Syrian mountains. It's obvious that the Israelis have taken the slopes. A gigantic fire is raging far beyond the crest, blotting out the nearby stars. It grows larger, and for a moment it seems as if the sun were trying to rise in the middle of the night.

June 10. "It was a miracle. No one on the kibbutz was even scratched," Aliza tells me. "Thirty boys were called up for the army, and we haven't heard a word from any of them yet, but the bunkers protected everyone here.

"It started last Monday, at exactly a quarter to ten. The small hand-siren went off, and in an instant the trenches were filled with people carrying kids to their assigned bunkers. I went to mine. We'd been practicing for three weeks, but this was the real thing, and everybody knew it. They all behaved beautifully.

"Then the shelling started. Sometimes there was

a whistle and a thud, and sometimes just a thud. The earth shook."

"Eighty-two mm mortars and 120 mm cannons," says Shlomo. "There were about forty hits within the area of the kibbutz itself, but no major damage. Come on and I'll show you."

At the silo, he collects a handful of razor-sharp metal fragments from a slight depression in the red earth.

"A mortar," he says. "Strictly antipersonnel. That'll give you some idea of what it can do to a human being."

He points to a concrete wall of the building pitted with deep holes.

"Have a look at this, in the field."

I'm wearing sandals. The thistles make it hard to walk.

"Just a little further," he says. "Right here."

It looks to me like a large gopher hole, dug obliquely into the ground.

On his hands and knees, Shlomo reaches in with his right arm, up to the shoulder, and shakes his head.

"I can't touch it. It's buried too deep."

"What is it?" I ask him. "Why is the hole all burned like that?"

"It's a dud," he says. "A 120 mm shell that didn't go off. There are a couple more down in the orchard, and one near the chicken coop. I'll have to dig them all up and defuse them."

He takes me through the new trenches that face the Syrian frontier. At one of the forward salients, reinforced by sandbags and covered with a sheet of corrugated iron, Amos is working furiously over a machine gun.

"The damned thing is jammed again," he says. "I just stripped it this morning."

"How are you?" I ask him.

"Good, and you? How's Marilyn?"

"Fine. She sends her best."

Shlomo and I go back. In an open wood shed—on top of a pile of bound bales of hay—a telescope has been set up. Gazing through it, at the slopes of the Syrian mountains, I can clearly see two Israeli Centurion tanks with their hatches open and their cannon pointing down. Greasy black smoke. The one on the right is on fire.

"What was that big fight last night?" I ask Shlomo.

"The breakthrough, on the plateau, to Quneitra. It's a fairly big city and was their GHQ for the whole area. Apparently that did it. I've heard that they've accepted a cease-fire for six-thirty tonight."

Through the telescope I can see three Centurions racing up the slopes.

"Where's the fighting now?" I ask.

"We're mopping up everywhere."

"Are the Syrians any good?"

"Some run and some fight like tigers. It took two hours of hand-to-hand fighting at Tel Azazyiat yesterday before they surrendered."

"Aliza wrote that you were out at night laying land mines."

"Did she?"

"Right under the Syrian positions."

"Why don't you go back to the room and get something cold to drink? I want to check that machine gun."

"He was out almost every night for three weeks before the war," Aliza tells me. "I know what he was doing, but he refused to talk about it. You know how he is. When the doctors told him he could postpone his appendix operation, he couldn't leave the hospital fast enough to get back here and 'go to work,' as he put it.

"Generally he got home about four. I couldn't sleep a wink. All I kept thinking about was a basket case I saw at Tel Hashomir, where Seymour got his prosthesis. Have you seen him yet, by the way? He's marvelous. Anyway, I kept thinking about this boy who was a mine expert, until one exploded in his face. He was blind, deaf, and dumb, with no arms, just little stumps, and legless way above the knees.

184

His jaw had been blown away, and he had no tongue. He was all I could think about every night, for three weeks, until Shlomo would finally come home and get into bed . . . Do you want some more iced coffee?"

"No, thanks."

"Have you seen our new refrigerator?"

"It's lovely."

"Isn't it, though. But the ice cubes are too small."

"Tell me more about the war."

"I only saw about ten minutes of it, early yesterday morning, during an all-clear, when we were allowed out of the shelters to watch our planes bombing the Syrian positions and our tanks attacking the fortifications. There are no roads up there, so they had unarmored bulldozers, from the kibbutzim in the area, make a path for them. When one got hit, they shoved it aside and brought up another to take its place. Then the siren went off, and we went down to the bunkers again. All told, we were there from Monday until this morning, just before you came. There were enough all-clears to allow the children to go to the toilets in the trenches and get a breath of fresh air. One night Edith even had enough time to cook chickens in the oven. We had stocked up enough food and water to last us three months, if necessary. But roast chicken! It was delicious.

"I was in charge of a bunker with eighteen adolescents and three babies from three weeks to four months old with their mothers. We all slept on twenty-one three-decker bunks, about a meter and a half long. We didn't sleep much. The mothers were terrified of rolling over and smothering their babies, and the older children wanted to go outside and watch the fireworks. It was some job controlling them. The girls giggled a lot.

"I was never actually frightened—there was so much to do—until one night Seymour rang up from the command bunker and asked if we had a man with us and a shovel. 'Why?' I asked him. 'I was just wondering,' he said. A few minutes later, during the shelling, one of the men arrived with a shovel. Then, all of a sudden, it occurred to me that he had been sent here in case a shell collapsed the entrance and we were buried alive. We would need a man to dig us out. I didn't panic, but, my God, when the all-clear sounded, it was good to be out in open air for a few minutes, under the stars."

Seymour drops by. Except for his missing middle finger—he's forced to hold a cigarette between his thumb and forefinger—and a pronounced limp, he seems well. When he leaves, Aliza tells me that he learned to use his prosthesis in almost half the time it usually takes.

"Including a horrible setback," she says. "One night, when he was still on crutches and on his way to the dining hall to see a film, he tripped and fell right on his stump. It was all black and blue—a massive internal hemorrhage, which had to be drawn off in the hospital."

Shlomo returns with Adi and Ruthie. In two years, she has become taller and more beautiful. Her face is thinner, dominated more than ever by her dark eyes. Proud of her figure, she wears brief shorts and a tight blouse with an embroidered collar. Not yet pubescent, Adi remains the image of his father, with his stocky build. They chatter away and laugh.

Aliza and Shlomo talk about the war, particularly the liberation of Jerusalem and the radio broadcast of the blowing of the shofar at the Wailing Wall.

"The Saba cried," she says. "To tell you the truth, so did I. So did a lot of people."

"That's all this country needs," says Shlomo. "A religious revival."

He says it so seriously, scowling, and the response is so predictable, that both Aliza and I burst out laughing.

The children go outside. "A couple of weeks ago, while he was studying the Bible for an exam, Adi asked me if I believed in God," says Aliza.

"What'd you tell him?" I ask.

" 'Sometimes.' I told him that sometimes, in spite of everything, I believed in something that was eternal and much greater than man."

"What'd he say to that?"

" 'Me too, Mama. So do I.' "

"It's six-thirty-five," says Shlomo, glancing at his wristwatch. "The cease-fire's been on for five minutes."

We leave the room. The lights in all the bungalows have been turned on.

"Off! Turn off all the lights! Black out!" Seymour calls out from down the path. "I just got a call."

We turn off the lights in the room, and Aliza methodically checks the contents of the canvas bag she had in the bunker during the war: one long-sleeved shirt, a pair of heavy work shoes, a paper bag filled with a flashlight, a pad of paper, two pencils, matches, four candles, a comb, and a deck of playing cards.

Shlomo comes in.

"Forget it," he tells her. "It was a false alarm."

"Are you sure?"

"Positive. Some idiot made a mistake. Let's go eat. Hugh can say hello to everybody."

Outside the dining hall at least ten Israeli flags have been run up on poles. Not a breeze. They all hang limply.

"How can you stand all those women kissing you?" Shlomo whispers to me while we eat. "I couldn't stand it."

After dinner we remain where we are. Bottles of beer and sweet wine are placed on all the tables. The room is crowded. Over thirty South African volunteers, all in their twenties, have been here since last Sunday, and will remain for at least three months to work.

The Saba is sitting across the room, smiling. He wears a black felt hat, with a round, stiff wide brim, a white shirt, black tie, a long gray double-breasted gabardine coat, and knee-length white stockings—the costume of a Hasid. His beard has been carefully combed into two points, and he looks younger and healthier than I've ever seen him. As a matter of fact, it's the first time I've seen him in the dining hall at a public function.

Aliza has told me that he was perfectly calm in his bunker, reciting his morning prayers with his phylacteries, which he keeps in a ragged, red velvet bag. His daughter carefully stored his separate dishes under his bunk, and a supply of tinned kosher meat. But he was perfectly content to live on dairy dishes— a little bit of kosher sour cream, cheese, bread, and butter.

David stands up and makes a brief speech about the origins of the war from what army intelligence has told him. He is much more formidable looking than I remember him, with his bushy eyebrows, broad chest, and slightly bandy, muscled legs. My Hebrew is rusty, and Edith Cohen must provide a running translation. She's so tired that she leans her head on her hands and speaks with her eyes closed. I listen desultorily—most of what David has to say, I've already read in the papers—until he makes two statements: one, that in the event of an early, concerted armored and infantry attack by the Syrians, the Galilee would have had to hold out on its own, without help from the army, for the first thirty-six hours; and two, that three weeks ago two highly trained battalions of one thousand Egyptian commandos were sent into Jordan with instructions to split Israel in half. It was their jump-off signal, in code, radioed from Egypt and intercepted by Israeli intelligence, that prompted Israel to attack Egypt on June 5th. Some of the commandos managed to infiltrate as far as ten miles from Tel Aviv before they were captured, and others are still at large.

A South African boy who has just entered the room lets the swinging door bang against a chair. Rama darts from beneath a table, quivering, with her ears back and her tail between her legs. Everyone laughs.

"She's a terrible coward," says Edith. "During the shelling she lay in one of the bunkers quivering like that the whole time. She drank a little water, but wouldn't eat anything."

"No wonder she looks so thin."

Amos, the new secretary of the kibbutz, stands up

and asks for a moment of silence for those who have fallen for their country. When he raises his head again, he pours himself a glass of beer and proposes a toast to peace.

We all drink. Edith and I sip beer from the same glass. "Don't cry," she tells me. "Please don't cry. Everything's all right now. Here's a hanky. Blow your nose."

Some of the South Africans turn on a phonograph and begin dancing a hora to *"Hava Nagila."* All the others leave to get some sleep.

"Look at the Syrian mountains," says Aliza. "No lights. Not a light anywhere up there for the first time in twenty years."

The dark peaks are silhouetted against the sky by the feeble light of the moon in its first quarter.

June 11. All day long we've been receiving messages from the boys in the army. Uri is safe, along with twenty-four others. Three have been wounded, and two are missing. As the day goes on, we get the details. One boy has been seriously wounded in the diaphragm by a bullet and has developed pneumonia. Another has been hit on the backside by shrapnel. The third in the back, by a sniper, in the streets of the Old City of Jerusalem, but miraculously the bullet passed through his flesh without causing any serious damage.

I don't think I know any of the wounded or missing. Some have become members of the kibbutz in the last two years, and I simply can't remember the others. At lunch, the wife of one of the missing boys stands at a table, wearing a blue apron, talking to Yora. Dark hair, a round face, now extraordinarily pale. I can't recall her either. Aliza has told me she has a year-old son.

After lunch I see Miriam Cohen on the path. She's still fat, but Edith says that she was finally able to persuade Hans and Lisel to let the girl see a woman psychotherapist in Haifa three times a week. She has been under treatment now for about a year. Her compulsive overeating is still a problem, but she suffers much less frequently from nightmares and will now undress in front of other girls her age.

"In the weeks before the war, she regressed very badly. An eight-year-old boy was kidnaped from Kibbutz Dan by the Syrians. God knows what they did to him. His body was never found. Miriam was a wreck. Once the shelling started, though, and she saw how all the other kids in her shelter behaved, she settled down and was fine.

"Lisel was icy calm. Three days before it all started, she found Hans's old Czech pistol and made him teach her how to use it. She had four bullets, but told me that two were enough. One for Miriam and one for herself, in case the kibbutz was overrun.

'Right through the temple,' she said. She always kept it with her in one of those canvas bags you sling over your shoulder."

At about three, Shlomo discovers that the army is holding twenty-six Syrian prisoners in the orchard. They were first brought to the police station in Kiriat Shemona, where a crowd of Jews from the Arab countries gathered and threatened to lynch them. Unable to handle the situation, the police asked the soldiers to bring them here.

We drive down to have a look. Two guards, armed with FN's, prevent us from getting too close. Hidden among the trees is a truck with a canvas roof filled with men. One stands up. His hands are tied behind his back, and his eyes are blindfolded. He's wearing a white shirt.

Explosions, and puffs of gray smoke on the slopes. It's Shlomo's guess that the army is blowing up the Syrian fortifications.

After dinner, I talk with Amir, a member of the kibbutz who interrogated the prisoners this afternoon. He was born and raised in Syria and speaks Arabic fluently. The author of several books for children, he is the headmaster of all the kibbutz high schools in the area.

"They were all captured from army villages, like Zaoura, or the fortifications, like Tel Azazyiat. The peasants, that is, the ordinary soldiers, the conscripts, were completely passive, inert, hardly responsive to anything. They said they were illiterate. Two of them finally spoke up a little. We were about to feed them —bread, tea, eggs—when one started to moan, 'I won't eat eggs. Eggs make me sick to my stomach. You can't make me eat eggs.' Another claimed to have just gotten out of the hospital with a broken leg and complained that if the doctors had kept the plaster cast on for a few more days he wouldn't be here now.

"The officers, who were intellectuals, or at least educated, were terrified we were going to shoot them. They said they had been given orders to spare no one and therefore had expected the same treatment. One of them was a philosophy student from the University of Damascus. When I asked him if he really believed all the propaganda on Radio Damascus about conquering Israel and exterminating the Jews, he thought a moment and then said no, not really, but he said he also never believed we'd be able to take the heights.

"Then there was a sixth-grade schoolteacher from Zaoura who claimed to be a civilian. He was in his middle twenties, but claimed he wasn't in the army because he was a teacher. He also said he remained behind when the fighting started to stay with his old parents. I asked him why they weren't evacuated, but he had no satisfactory explanation. He kept repeating he was worried because he didn't know what had happened to them. Then I asked him what he taught his people about Israel and the Israelis, and just like that he answered, 'Probably similar to what you teach yours about us.' He was so quick and shrewd I had to laugh. But I had the feeling that he was lying and was probably an officer in mufti. Maybe in Intelligence . . . I had the feeling they were all lying, to one degree or another, about something, in the hope that it might somehow help them. A cloud of lies, little ones, big ones, like ink squirted from a squid, to hide behind . . .''

I get a chance this evening to have a few words with Aaron Stern, who left Rehovoth to return to help defend the kibbutz during the war and is now, aided by the South African volunteers, working desperately in the cotton fields to save the crop, which has been left unweeded for two weeks.

"Have you seen the trees?" he asks me.

"Yes. They've grown. Filled out. How's school?"

"All right."

June 12. A postcard has been tacked up in the dining hall from one of the wounded boys who is at the

Hadassah Hospital in Jerusalem. He sends greetings to all the members of the kibbutz but is sorry to say that he wasn't wounded in the bottom, as first reported, but a little higher up. He's receiving wonderful care and thanks all those who sent him fruit and flowers and took the time to write him. He hopes to be able to write his next note himself. "Please find me an easy job in the secretariat's office," he says, "as I will now be useless in the cowshed."

"We called the hospital," Aliza says. "He has shrapnel in his neck, which damaged his spinal column. He can't move his hands at all, but the doctor assures us that he'll gradually regain use of them. There's still no word from any of the missing."

The Chink sits at a table with a particularly hang-dog look.

"He's got problems," says Aliza. "His mother-in-law, who must be in her seventies, was living all alone in Tel Aviv and asked if she couldn't come and live here to be near her daughter. We never refuse a request like that. So we fixed up a decent room for her and she came. But she didn't like it. She was frightened of being alone at night. She moved into the Chink's room, and he had to move into hers. His wife insisted. Now he sleeps all alone, and his wife and mother-in-law share the same bed."

As school resumes tomorrow, Nat is busy in his room preparing the first lesson. I hardly recognize him. He has shaved off his mustache, revealing a long upper lip. As though an impediment has been corrected, or perhaps because I can see his lips move as he speaks, he seems to enunciate more clearly.

"It's very hard," he says. "I want to talk to them about the consequences of the war and explain that all we want is to sign a peace treaty with the Arabs. But if they don't do it, we'll have to continue to occupy Sinai, the west bank of the Jordan, and the Syrian heights, for our own protection. And this means that we'll be regarded as conquerors by a million resentful Arabs. If they actively resist us and resort to terror, we'll have to retaliate . . .

"But I've also got to make them understand that we have a special responsibility to be as just and merciful as possible. Our history demands it. All the anguish of the Diaspora. If we became oppressors now, after all of that, it would be a betrayal of everything that we . . ."

But he breaks off, with his eyes shut. They are sunk in their sockets.

"What about Jerusalem?" I ask.

"What about it?"

"You didn't mention giving that up."

"No," he says. "And we never will. It's our historic capital. And then there's the Wall . . ."

"What do you care about the Wall if you're not religious?"

He gives me a startled look. "Yes. I've been thinking about that. When we captured it I wept without knowing why. Why did the early Zionists, who were atheists, insist on returning here? Herzl, as you know, was offered Uganda as a Jewish national home, but the Sixth Zionist Congress refused to consider it. It had to be *Eretz*, or nothing.

". . . It was as if they unconsciously assumed that a covenant between the Jews and God still existed," he goes on, after a pause. "And sometimes I feel that deep down we feel the same way. It's depressing. You'd think that by now we'd be finished with Him once and for all . . ."

He absently raises his forefinger and strokes his clean-shaven upper lip.

"But is it possible to create a humane civilization without Him?" he says. "That's the question . . ."

At nine-thirty in the evening, Amos comes into the dining hall, where eight of us have been talking, and announces, "Shimon has died in the hospital."

Everyone rises and leaves without a word.

"What is it? What's happened?" I ask Edith. Although I understood the Hebrew sentence perfectly, for an instant I was incapable of assimilating its meaning. Shimon was the boy who had been wounded in the diaphragm.

We go to the Wolfes's room where Shlomo turns on his stereo tape recorder—a resonant organ plays Bach's *Passacaglia and Fugue in C Minor*.

"Do you hear the difference?" he asks me. "A beautiful tone. It's new. A Crossfield."

"I hadn't noticed."

"I traded in my Grundig and my old Leica and paid the difference in cash. It cleaned us out, but it's worth it, don't you think?"

"The tone is beautiful."

Edith and I sit together on the convertible sofa, Aliza in a chair to our right. We're joined by Seymour, Yora, and finally Nat, who has brought along a copy of *Maariv*. He opens it as soon as he sits down and reads the news. Only Ruthie, standing in a corner, makes a sound. She weeps quietly, wipes her eyes, regains control of herself, and then weeps again, until she takes a deep breath.

"Shimon was the leader of her group," Edith explains. Her voice is hoarse from fatigue and smoking. "All the kids adored him."

The *Toccata, Adagio and Fugue in C Major* resounds in the small room. "Make it lower," Aliza tells her husband. Instead, he takes two bottles of liquor down from the closet—a half-gallon of Johnny Walker Red, which I bought in the Zurich airport, and a pint of Vishniak, Israeli sweet cherry brandy. He pours stiff shots of Scotch for Edith, Seymour, and himself and looks inquiringly at me. I shake my head.

Nat and Aliza sip a little brandy. Ruthie weeps again until her father whispers something in her ear.

Then she laughs, blows her nose, and puts on a pair of dark glasses.

By ten-thirty, Shlomo, Aliza, and I have been left alone. A knock on the door. It's Esther, the nurse, breathless from excitement. She tells us that her husband has just returned home from the army and insists that we come over for a few minutes to say shalom.

The man, who obviously doesn't remember me, shakes my hand. His khaki shirt is torn at the right elbow. Filthy, unshaven, with a bad cold, he tells us that he was at Sharm el Sheikh where the Egyptians deserted their bunkers, escaped into the desert, and then returned to surrender.

He coughs. Exhaustion has made him thick-tongued, and he sounds as if he were drunk.

He says that he has it on good authority that the Egyptians on the other side of the Suez Canal machine-gunned their own troops who had managed to straggle across the desert.

His wife, who has been unlacing his boots, raises her head.

"But why?"

"To prevent them from spreading the truth . . . Who knows?" He shrugs.

June 13. All the Israeli flags have been taken down in front of the dining hall, and inside, within a glass case opposite the door, is a photograph of Shimon, framed in black paper. It's an enlarged snapshot of him sitting crosslegged on the lawn in front of his room. Dark eyes, dark hair, and a mustache.

Except for the soldiers, who are camped near the orchard and are lounging everywhere, the kibbutz seems to have returned to normal. The men are back at their various jobs, and the women are particularly busy cleaning up and doing the accumulated laundry, after five days in the bunkers.

Edith is helping out in the infants' house, preparing formulas for three babies who lie on reed mats on the tile floor, sucking pacifiers. One of them is Shimon's four-month-old son.

"Where's Elana?" I ask her. "I haven't seen her around."

"She was here during the war, but rushed back to Jerusalem immediately afterward. The morning you arrived. The kibbutz sent her there to study for two years at the Bezalel Art School, with the understanding that when she comes back she'll teach art to the kids here. She's doing very well. She's become very interested in woodcuts and lithography."

"Send her my love."

"Of course."

Aliza comes in with a pile of clean infants' clothes she's collected from one of the bunkers and begins sorting them out.

"Shlomo thinks that both Yaakov and Yehuda are dead."

"Why?"

"He says that we should have heard something from them by this time. Yaakov's unit is now somewhere up in Syria, and Shlomo and Amos want to go up and check. I begged them not to. One of the officers told me after breakfast that it's absolutely forbidden unless you have a special pass. Three Israeli soldiers had their throats cut last night, and there's still sniping going on, and mines. Two boys were killed at dawn this morning. They went over a mine in a jeep."

A *khamsin* today, which, with the four hours sleep a night that I've been getting in the last few days, completely enervates me. Returning to the Wolfes's room at noon to take a nap, I run into Shlomo. He's in uniform—boots, leopard-skin camouflage pants, and a khaki shirt with the insignia of a lieutenant on his shoulders. Over one arm he carries another khaki shirt and pair of pants.

"Do you want to go up?" he asks me.

"Of course."

"Then put these on, and for God's sake keep your mouth shut."

Amos is already in the covered jeep next to the driver's seat with two Uzis beside him.

"You won't get any lunch," Aliza cries out.

"Never mind," her husband tells her, spreading handfuls of red earth on the jeep's hood, and lightly spraying it with a hose. It's the standard camouflage used on almost all the light Israeli vehicles I've seen on the way to the front.

I get into the back and brace my legs. Aliza waves. Her face is pale and contracted as though she were suffering from a violent headache. We drive away.

Although we were never friends, I suddenly have distinct memories of Yaakov from two years ago. For some reason, I picture him seated on the edge of a table in the dining hall, with one leg drawn up and his chin resting on his knees. He's squinting. Was he myopic?

Beyond Kfar Szold we make a right, and on a rutted dirt track begin to climb the Syrian heights, raising clouds of red dust. The slope is so steep that we're almost vertical, and I have to hang on to the back of Amos' seat with both hands. Then Shlomo stops, and the dust settles. Below us is a white shack —OP Alpha, the deserted UN Observation Post. A door has been left open. We're in Syria, or what was formerly Syria, surrounded by ripe wheat.

Off again. The dust clogs my nostrils. Another stop. To the left, just behind us, the burned-out hull of an Israeli half-track that exploded. Ammunition cases, spent cartridges, and burned pieces of paper are scattered about, among the wheat, for a hundred yards.

"Here."

Shlomo holds up a steel helmet that has been perforated through the crown.

"Keep it as a souvenir," he tells me.

"No thanks."

He throws it away and drives on, higher, until he stops again.

"There you are. Straight down there. The back of Tel Azazyiat."

I can see only a concrete turret and the twisted branches of an olive tree.

"Can we get any closer?" I ask.

"Not on your life. You see those white tapes strung everywhere? Mines."

"How did they miss anything?" says Amos. "That's what I want to know. You can piss and hit anything in the whole valley from there."

Again, as we go on, the dust hides my view, but the Hula Valley spread out behind us remains in my mind: the cultivated fields, the trees, buildings, and, in the distance, like rectangular mirrors set into the earth to reflect the blue sky, the artificial fish ponds.

"The sight must have driven them crazy," Shlomo yells over the roar of the motor. "No wonder they hate us so much . . ."

We finally reach the summit of the plateau and a

paved road that leads directly into Quneitra. More wheatfields, as far as the eye can see, divided by low fences made from black volcanic rock.

"They had to sow and reap all of that by hand," says Shlomo.

"How can you tell?"

"The plots are too small. You can't get machinery in there."

An MP armed with an Uzi waves us to a halt. I slump down, with my arms crossed on my chest and my eyes closed.

"What'd he want?" I ask, when we're allowed to continue.

"He warned us against looting and wanted to see my special pass."

"What'd you tell him?"

"The truth. That we were trying to find out what happened to a friend."

A dead dog is lying on the side of the road. We slow down to avoid the carcass of a donkey with a swollen stomach. Two more dogs. The large brown one, on the right, has its mouth open. Its tongue lolls to one side. Another donkey, a colt, with a distended stomach. Suddenly the brown dog gets up, stretches, with its forepaws extended, its rump in the air—it has a bushy tail—and trots off.

"The dog got up."

"What's that?"

"The brown dog's alive."

"I can't hear you," Shlomo yells. "The wind. What did you say? Did I hit a dog?"

"No, no . . ."

Quneitra, on the deserted main street. Above the red tile roofs of the stone buildings and shuttered shops, a white minaret. We pass a movie, advertising some Arabic film with a colored poster, half of which has been torn from the wall. Only the picture of a handsome, dark-haired man remains, holding out his left hand. A white rag on the end of a stick hangs from a balcony on which an Israeli soldier is seated, with his boots on the iron balustrade.

We park in front of the municipal police station, now Israeli army GHQ. The place has been bombed, and although the concrete façade is intact, all the windows have been blown out. Fragments of glass, rolls of toilet paper, Arab magazines litter the street.

"We're going inside to check," says Shlomo.

"Okay, I'll stay here."

"Don't speak English with anyone."

I climb down. At my feet is a large, framed photograph covered by a cracked pane of glass of a Syrian mother and her two sons. The woman is very old, dressed in black, with a black shawl over her head, but still very beautiful. She has delicate features and large, clear eyes. The boys are in their early twenties. The one on the left is bare-headed and wears a double-breasted suit. His brother has a long *kaffiah*, with an *argal*, draped around his head. They gaze into the camera with much more diffidence than the old woman, whose look shows her love and pride. I glance around—no one is watching—smash the glass, and then the wooden frame.

"That's a souvenir worth keeping," says Shlomo.

"Yes, I'll keep it."

He hands me a bottle of orange soda, which I gulp down without taking a breath.

"What about Yaakov? Any news?"

"His unit may be at Nafach or Sindiana. We have to go on."

We drive out of town to a junction; north, perhaps fifty miles away, or even less, is Damascus. The road is empty, guarded by two MP's. We head south. The landscape is beginning to change. In the distance are the eroded craters of extinct volcanoes. We turn off, onto another dusty track.

"Nafach," says Shlomo.

We pull up under a grove of eucalyptus trees. Israeli soldiers are sleeping in the shade.

"Well?" I ask Shlomo, when he returns from the CP.

"Not here."

"Are you going to Fiq?" a fat soldier calls out.

"Maybe," Shlomo tells him.

He climbs into the back with me, and under way again we talk in English. He tells me that he's an insurance agent in Tel Aviv and a tank-maintenance man in the reserve. He went up the Syrian slopes during the battle on Friday, following the armor.

"It was the first combat I'd ever seen," he says. "And I didn't think I'd make it. I was sure I wouldn't make it."

"Are you married?"

"Engaged."

"Congratulations."

"I never thought I'd make it," he repeats, biting his thumbnail.

Another camp. Tents in another grove of eucalyptus trees. Amos and Shlomo go to inquire about Yaakov's unit while the fat soldier and I wander around in the shade. We come to a pit filled with six prisoners dressed in ragged khaki uniforms. They all have their hands tied behind their backs and are blindfolded with fringed *kaffiahs*. A Yemenite corporal stands over them with an Uzi. Darker than the Arabs, with coffee-colored skin, he wears a beard and ear-locks. On the back of his head is a straw cowboy's hat.

We move closer. The prisoners lie on their backs or sides, motionless. One of them has been wounded in the right foot, which is bound in bloody rags. The man next to him suddenly raises his head to moan,

"*Yah Allah! Yah Allah!*"—again and again.

"If it was up to me, I'd shoot them all," says the fat soldier.

Back to the jeep. "Sindiana, definitely," says Shlomo.

Here and there, in the wheat, a live donkey, and then a cow who has sensed that human beings are passing on the road. She lumbers toward us, and I can see that her udders are full.

We are forced to wait for almost fifteen minutes while a ragged crowd of fifty or sixty Syrian peasant women and children are herded across the road by four Israeli soldiers. Some of the children are naked. All of the women are barefoot and wear identical shapeless black dresses and shawls sewn with strings of silver coins that dangle on their foreheads. A suckling infant wails. Its mother carries a folded mattress on her head. The women are loaded down with their possessions: pots and pans, brass trays and coffee pots, clay jugs, a glazed blue vase, bundles of clothing wrapped in blankets. They have obviously just been expelled from their village—mud huts set back two hundred yards or so, on our right.

"Where're they taking them?" I ask Shlomo.

"To their own lines."

"But where're the men?"

"Interned."

"What about him?"

"Who?"

"The one in his undershorts."

Shlomo turns around. Behind us, less than ten yards away, a Syrian squats on his haunches, with his hands clasped on his head, guarded by an Israeli soldier. The Syrian shifts his weight, and the soldier raises the muzzle of his FN.

"Who's he?" I ask.

"How should I know?" says Shlomo. "A sniper, maybe, or a terrorist."

With the muzzle now pressed against his right temple, the Syrian lifts his head and our eyes meet. He's young, in his mid-twenties, with broad shoulders and thick black tufts of hair under his arms. The jeep suddenly lurches forward, but we continue to look each other in the eye. Then he spits.

At Sindiana, Shlomo and Amos leap out of the jeep and shake hands with a short officer. He clasps them both around the back of the neck, lowers his head to listen to their questions, and then replies for almost a minute. Shlomo nods.

"He's dead," Amos comes over to tell me. "Napalmed by our own planes."

"Where? How did it happen?"

"At Jenin. He was part of an advance patrol that discovered some Jordanian Pattons and called an air strike down on them. Only they were too close and got it too." He spreads his hands. "About this much of him was left. About a meter."

When we're on our way again, Shlomo continues south, toward the Sea of Galilee, rather than returning to the kibbutz the way we came.

"We need time," he tells me. "We've got to think of the best way to tell his wife."

"The details?"

"No, of course not."

He slows down. A young, barefoot Syrian peasant, dressed in a white shirt and blue pants, lies in the center of the road. His eyes are closed, and with his head resting on his outstretched arm, he appears to have fallen asleep. Now a burned-out Russian jeep and the bodies of five soldiers scattered around it. One lies directly in our path, and Shlomo swerves around him. His face is charred black, but his mouth is open and I can see his upper teeth. The fire has seared the inside of his left leg and crotch, but the other leg and his stomach are untouched. Something —a buckle?—glitters.

Seven more bodies in the middle of the road that have become so bloated in the heat that their distended uniforms seem about to burst. The leather belt of one on the left has already snapped. His right hand is raised, the fingers widely spread. It resembles an inflated glove. The flesh has turned yellow. A tremendous fart. I look around. The fat soldier is talking with Shlomo and Amos. Another fart, as we drive away, and I realize that it's gas escaping from the rectum of one of the corpses.

By the time we return to the kibbutz, it's eight o'clock. Shlomo and I walk up the path to his room past one of the children's houses.

"There she is," he whispers. "In the window."

"Who?"

"Yaakov's wife. No, don't look up. I don't want to talk to her now. She sees us. Keep going . . . Quick!"

"What took you so long?" says Aliza. "I was worried sick."

"We went all the way down to the other side of the Sea of Galilee," I tell her. "And then north again, where we crossed the Jordan into Israel at the Benot Yaakov bridge."

I hold up the photo of the Arab family that we hid under Amos' seat before we were searched by the MP as we left Syria.

"How could you?" she says. "That's horrible. Throw it away."

I tear the picture into shreds and toss it into the plastic garbage can in the toilet.

"But you must," Aliza is saying to Shlomo when I go back into the room. "She's been waiting all day.

She already knows he's dead. Five minutes after you left here, an officer from his unit came and told her. All you have to do is say a few kind words."

"Like what?"

"I don't know. You'll think of something."

"It's not my responsibility. Amos is secretary of the kibbutz."

"Shlomo, you have to go and see her for a few minutes."

"Well, I'm going to get cleaned up first."

"Are you hungry?" Aliza asks me.

"Starved."

"Take a shower, change your clothes, and I'll make you some eggs. How does that sound?"

"Wonderful."

We devour the fried eggs, white cheese, white bread, butter, sliced tomatoes, and drink two glasses of iced coffee each. When Shlomo is finished, he gets up and goes out the door.

"Yaakov had a year-old son," Aliza says.

"I know. You told me."

"Did I? Yehuda is also dead. We got word this afternoon. He was killed in Jerusalem."

"Married?"

"Oh no, he was very young."

Three-quarters of an hour later Shlomo returns, saying nothing.

June 14. Two more photos, framed by black paper, in the glass case in the dining hall. I recognize Yaakov immediately. The photo shows him without glasses. Yehuda is very young, thin and blond. His picture, taken from a distance, against a background of bushes, makes it hard for me to distinguish his features.

Aliza has told me that although the kibbutz will hold no religious service for the dead, it will go into mourning for two weeks in which all public festivities, such as parties or movies, will be canceled.

With Amos and Shlomo in the Wolfes's room. Amos is looking through a Hebrew biblical atlas and has come upon a map of the Davidic and Solomaic kingdoms—the most extensive Jewish occupation of Palestine up to the present time.

"Not bad. According to this, we not only had both sides of the Jordan, but went right up to the Tigris and Euphrates as well."

"How long did it last?" Shlomo asks.

Amos laughs. "Idiot! What's the difference? Don't you understand that it makes no difference?"

When he leaves, Shlomo studies the map for a moment and then replaces the book on the shelf. The room is filled with the merciless light of the sun. Has he changed so much since I was last here? He's now forty. His hair is a little thinner, and he's put on weight around his middle.

"If the Arabs won't sit down and negotiate a peace treaty with us, we'll probably have to do it all over again in another five or ten years," he says. "Ah, what the hell . . ."

Left alone for a while, I come across Adi's copybook for his English lessons. He prints in a large, awkward hand on the lined paper. The last entry is dated yesterday.

The War.

Last week we had a war. Israel had to fight Egypt, Jaardan, Iraq, and Syria. We won, but many soldiers are dead and nany are wounded. The Arabs had many tanks, aerplanes, guns and bambs. But our men are better. Now we are happy and sad at the same time.

About the Author

HUGH NISSENSON was born in 1933 in New York City. He attended Fieldston School and Swarthmore College, from which he graduated Phi Beta Kappa, and was a Wallace Stegner Literary Fellow at Stanford University. He has written short stories published in *Commentary*, *Harper's*, *Playboy*, *Esquire*, and other magazines, and reported on the Eichmann trial for *Commentary*. A collection of his stories, *A Pile of Stones*, was published in 1965 and won the Edward Lewis Wallant Award as the best book of that year of American-Jewish significance.

PENSACOLA JUNIOR COLLEGE LIBRARY
HX765.P3 N57
Nissenson, Hugh.   000
Notes from the frontier.   210101

3 5101 00023030 5

HX765.P3N57   49,019

Nissenson, Hugh
Notes from the frontier

PENSACOLA JR. COLLEGE LIBRARY